LEON

HAPPY FAST FOOD

BY REBECCA SEAL, JACK BURKE
& JOHN VINCENT

cONTENTs

INTRODUCTION

Our *LEON Happy* series of cookbooks is all about nourishing the soul with food that nourishes the body. And making us happy as a result.

The truth is that, for many of us, time is short and, when we need something now, like *right now*, we're guilty of reaching for food that's not as good for us: greasy takeouts, sad microwave meals or TV dinners, and someone pass the cookie jar while you're at it.

But at LEON, we've always believed fast food doesn't have to be bad food. Since 2004, we've been serving up food that tastes good and does you good in double quick time. And now here's a cookbook that helps you do the same.

We've eaten our way around the world, gathering the best fast food recipes as we traveled, to give you a book of all our favorites made "good for you." And we've played fast and loose with the definition of fast food. Yes, you'll have burgers and fries and wraps, but you'll also have food that you can make fast (and that'll make you happy), such as pastas and salads and ice creams. Because every meal deserves to be an adventure in flavor, we have the classics and we have a few surprises: a Zucchini, Walnut & Mint "Cheese" Sandwich, a Paneer & Beet Wrap, and Roast Garlic Hummus.

Let's celebrate food that's colorful, delicious, and full of micronutrients. And fast.

Rebecca, Jack and John

KEY

WF
WHEAT FREE

GF
GLUTEN FREE

DF
DAIRY FREE

V
VEGETARIAN

Ve
VEGAN

NF
NUT FREE

SoF
SOY FREE

SUITABLE FOR FREEZING

LOSE THE PLASTIC

Sustainability is important to us at LEON, and we are always looking for ways to cut down waste and recycle more—we recently launched a program to recycle coffee cups (as well as selling reusable ones). Rebecca, who coauthored this book, and her husband became equally obsessed after watching a documentary about plastic, and this book marks the first (of her eight cookbooks) written using as little plastic packaging as possible.

The process has been a long way from perfect—there are plenty of things, such as store-bought bread crumbs and frozen peas, you just can't get without plastic—but we have cut waste by buying loose wherever possible. While it seemed difficult at first, we all feel that it is really important to do our part, and we have some suggestions for how you can, too. Remember, every change, however small, can make a difference:

• Get a load of durable containers with lids and use permanent ink to mark the tops and bottoms so you can always match the lids to the containers. Then, carry some with you to fill, along with a reusable shopping bag.

• Find a packaging-free store and visit every week or two. Rebecca takes her containers to buy in bulk dried goods, such as rice, flours, breakfast cereals, lentils, and pasta; oils, vinegars, and soy sauce; and rinse aid and dishwashing detergents.

• Make weekly shopping lists on a white board attached to the refrigerator instead of buying what you need from expensive convenience stores every day.

• Although some are catching up and moving to loose, avoid grocery stores when buying meat, fish, vegetables, and cheese to cut down on packaging — you can take your own containers to the local butcher or green grocer. Perhaps the best part is that you'll also reconnect with independent stores and the people who work there. We found that we ended up buying smaller quantities of things instead of being forced to buy big plastic trays of a predetermined size.

PANTRY

HERBS & SPICES

dried oregano	nutmeg	sumac	cayenne pepper
cumin	allspice	chili powder	turmeric
coriander	Chinese five-spice	paprika & smoked paprika	garlic & onion powders
nigella	cinnamon	dried red pepper flakes	fennel seeds

FREEZER

hamburger buns

flatbreads & wraps

good-quality naan

English muffins

peas

corn kernels

edamame (soybeans)

mixed berries

fish sticks

fries

REFRIGERATOR

capers in liquid	cheddar cheese
dill pickles	feta cheese
Indian pickles & chutneys	paneer
hot sauces	parmesan cheese
chipotle paste	mustard
harissa	English mustard
butter or vegan butter	Dijon mustard
milk or plant-based milk	tofu
yogurt	mayo

FRESH

sourdough bread

eggs

red & white onions

scallions

garlic

ginger

chilies

fennel

beets

cabbage

carrots

tomatoes

cucumber

radishes

crisp lettuce

soft leafy greens

fresh herbs (in flowerpots, if possible)

avocado

pomegranate

unwaxed citrus fruit

fresh fruit

CUPBOARD

neutral cooking oil (such as canola)

extra virgin olive oil

black pepper & flaky sea salt

rice vinegar

red wine vinegar

apple cider vinegar

sherry vinegar

canned black beans

canned chickpeas (garbanzo beans)

canned kidney beans

lentils

tomato puree or tomato sauce

ketchup

soy sauce

tahini

curry pastes

good-quality pasta

sushi rice

black rice

basmati

jasmine rice

quinoa

store-bought bread crumbs

plain/gluten-free flour

chickpea (besan) flour

oats

almond meal

crispy fried onions

nut & seeds

dried wakame & hijiki seaweeds

canned unripe green jackfruit

agave syrup

honey

semisweet & bittersweet chocolate

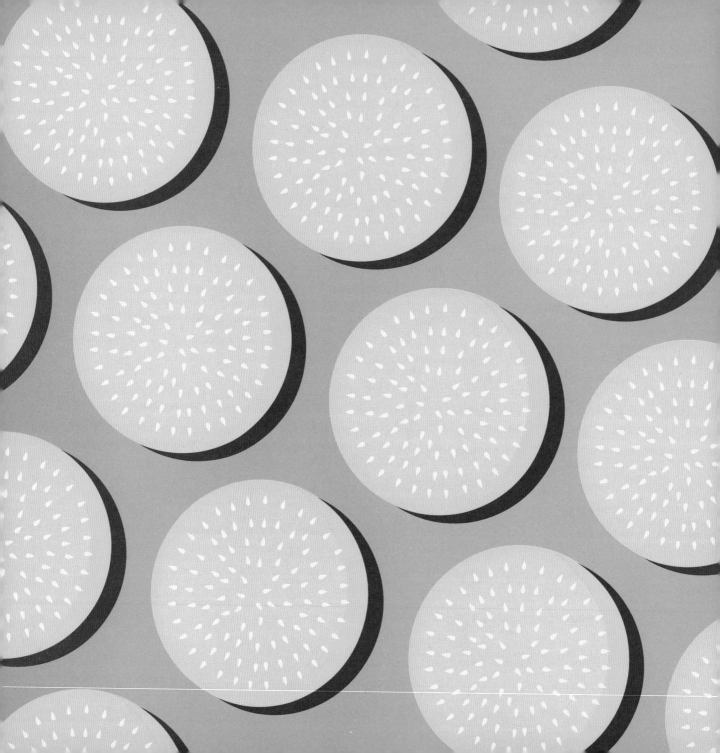

BREADS & ROLLS

A SUPER SIMPLE HAMBURGER

SERVES 4

PREP TIME: 10 MIN ∗ COOK TIME: 5–10 MIN

DF | NF | SoF

FOR THE BURGERS:

1 lb good-quality **ground round beef** (not low fat)

a little **sunflower** or **canola oil** (optional)

salt and **freshly ground black pepper**

TO SERVE:

4 large or 8 smaller **burger buns**, sliced in half and warmed or toasted

Mayo (of your choice), **Carolina Mustard Mayo**, or **LEON Burger Sauce** (see pages 188–190 and 193), or all three

shredded or whole **crisp lettuce leaves**

slices of **beefsteak tomato**

hamburger relish or **Thom's BBQ Sauce** (see page 191)

Dill Pickles (see page 185), sliced

Crispy Baked Fries (see page 173) and **Slaw** (see pages 95–97), to serve

We did a lot of (onerous, backbreaking) research, trying to work out how to make at home the kind of burger you get in fancy burger restaurants. But, in the end, we realized you can make great hamburgers with nothing but beef. No bread crumbs. No herbs. No egg. No onion. (Which is not how we'd been making them at home. Oops.) Have a go. We think you will see what we mean.

Before cooking the hamburger patties, get all your fillings and sides ready.

Divide the ground beef into four or eight equal portions, depending on the size of your buns. Shape into patties about ½ inch thick, working the meat as little as possible—overworking the beef makes burgers that are tight and bouncy in texture instead of juicy. Press a dimple into the center of each one, which will help the meat keep its patty shape instead of doming into a meatball during cooking.

Just before cooking, season each patty generously with salt and pepper (don't add salt to the meat before shaping). You can barbecue, grill, or pan-fry the patties. If you are using supermarket ground beef, cook the patties until well done. Only cook them rare or medium if the meat has been freshly ground by a butcher you trust.

Cook the patties briskly over high heat, with a little oil if using a pan, until done to your liking (about 2 minutes on each side, for us), turning so that both sides are deep brown. Don't press them with the spatula, because that squeezes out the lovely juices. Remove the patties from the heat and let rest for a couple of minutes.

Meanwhile, start building the burgers: lay out your warmed or toasted burger buns, place some mayo or burger sauce on each bottom half, then add some lettuce and a slice of tomato. Top this with a rested burger patty, relish or BBQ sauce, pickles, and the top of the bun. Serve with fries and slaw.

LOVε AT-HOME VEGAN BURGER

SERVES 6 (UNLESS STACKING DOUBLES!)
PREP TIME: 20 MIN ✳ COOK TIME: 40 MIN
DF | V | Ve

8 oz **extra-firm tofu**

2–3 tablespoons **vegetable oil**

1 large raw **beet**, peeled and finely shredded (¾ cup prepared)

1 **onion**, minced

1 clove of **garlic**, finely chopped

1 tablespoon ground **flaxseed**

3 tablespoons ground **walnuts**

3½ tablespoons **panko bread crumbs**

2 tablespoons cooked **black rice** (optional)

2 tablespoons **chickpea (besan) flour**

1 tablespoon **soy sauce**

½ teaspoon **Marmite**

½ teaspoon **vegan gravy powder**

TO SERVE:

6 **vegan burger buns**, sliced in half and warmed or toasted

Vegan Mayo or **Vegan Carolina Mustard Mayo** (see pages 190 and 189)

Dill Pickles (see page 185), sliced into rounds

1 large ripe **tomato**, sliced into 6 rounds

6 vegan **American cheese-style slices**

6 **Cos lettuce leaves**

hamburger relish or **Thom's BBQ Sauce** (see page 191)

Crispy Baked Fries (see page 173), to serve

A make-at-home version of our much-loved vegan LOVε burger. This version uses tofu, which isn't in our restaurant recipe but works to bind the patties for pan-frying, along with chickpea flour, walnuts, and flaxseed.

Wrap the tofu in a clean dish towel and gently squeeze out some of the excess liquid, then put it onto a plate and put another plate on top to squeeze out some more. Put a wide skillet over medium heat and add 1 tablespoon of the oil. When hot, add the beet and onion. Cook, stirring often, for 6–8 minutes. At this point, the vegetables may start to caramelize—reduce the heat to stop them from scorching and cook for another 6 minutes, until the beet has darkened and the onion is translucent. Add the garlic and cook, stirring, for another 2 minutes.

Meanwhile, mix the ground flaxseed with 2 tablespoons of water and let soak for 5 minutes. Process the tofu in a food processor until it becomes the texture of a soft pâté. Put it into a bowl with the walnuts, soaked flaxseed, bread crumbs, rice, if using, chickpea flour, soy sauce, Marmite, and gravy powder. When the vegetables in the pan are done, transfer them to the bowl and mix everything thoroughly.

To cook, wipe out the skillet, set it over medium heat, and add a tablespoon of oil. When hot, divide the mixture into six and shape into patties, about ½ inch thick. Cook in the hot oil for 4–5 minutes, until deep golden on the bottom. You might have to do this in batches. Don't move them around too much, because they are fragile at this point. When browned, carefully flip over and cook the other side.

Assemble each burger in this order: warm bun bottom half, mayo, pickles, tomato, lettuce, patty, cheese. Spread some burger relish or sauce on the top half of the bun, then rest it on the cheese. Serve with baked fries.

TIP

Don't be tempted to make thicker patties, because they will be squishy, and not in a good way. The cooked patties can be frozen for up to a month.

THAI-SPICED CORN BURGER

SERVES 4

PREP TIME: 15 MIN * COOK TIME: 15 MIN

DF | V | SoF

FOR THE BURGERS:

1 cup frozen **corn kernels**

½ teaspoon **ground cumin**

1½ tablespoons **Thai red curry paste**

6 fresh lime leaves, minced

2 **scallions**, finely chopped

1 tablespoon finely chopped **fresh cilantro leaves**

½ cup **green beans** (¼-inch pieces)

1 teaspoon finely chopped **red chili**

½ cup **chickpea (besan) flour**

½ teaspoon **baking powder**

1 teaspoon **freshly squeezed lime juice**

neutral cooking oil

salt and **freshly ground black pepper**

TO SERVE:

thinly sliced **cucumber**

1 small **carrot**, sliced into thin matchsticks

1 teaspoon finely chopped **red chili**

1 small **shallot**, as finely sliced as possible

freshly squeezed lime juice

a generous pinch of **superfine sugar**

mayo or **kewpie mayo**

4 **burger buns**, sliced in half and toasted

1 tablespoon chopped **unroasted peanuts**

sweet chili sauce or **Sriracha**

a small bunch of **fresh cilantro**

crisp lettuce, chopped

Here, we are stealing the spices (and most of the ingredients, in truth) from Thai fish cakes but making them into vegan corn burgers.

Bring a saucepan of water to a boil, add the corn, bring back to a boil, then drain. Set aside about one third of the corn in a bowl and put the remainder into a food processor. Add the cumin, curry paste, and lime leaves and process, scraping down the sides once or twice, to form a paste.

Add the scallions, cilantro, green beans and chili to the corn in the bowl and mix, then add the corn paste to the bowl. Add the chickpea flour, baking powder, lime juice, and 2 tablespoons of water. Season well and mix together into a thick batter that drops off a spoon, adding a dash more water, if needed.

Pour about 1½ tablespoons of oil into a wide skillet over medium-low heat. When shimmering hot, cook a nugget of the batter for a minute or two on each side. Taste to check the seasoning and heat level.

Divide the mix into four patties, each about 4 inches across. Add two to the hot pan, then cook for 3–4 minutes, until deep golden on the bottom—turn the heat to low if they are browning any faster. Carefully flip them over and cook the other side for about 3 minutes, until deep golden. Remove, keep warm, and repeat to cook the remaining two patties, adding more oil as needed.

Put the cucumber, carrot, chili, shallot, lime juice, and sugar into a small bowl and toss together.

Spread a little mayo or kewpie on the bottom of each bun, then add a quarter of the dressed veg and a pinch of the chopped nuts. Add a patty, then drizzle over a little sweet chili sauce or Sriracha. Finish with cilantro, lettuce leaves, and the bun tops.

SPICED LAMB BURGER

SERVES 4

PREP TIME: 20 MIN * COOK TIME: 15 MIN

NF | SoF

We've stolen the spicing from Eastern Mediterranean-style kofte and made them into a tasty burger instead. If you love the lamb kofte we sometimes have on the menu, then look out for the full recipe in our 2017 book, "Fast & Free".

olive or **vegetable oil**

½ small **onion**, minced

1 clove of **garlic**, crushed

1¼ lb good-quality **ground lamb** (choose one with more than 10 percent fat)

1 slice of **bread**, crusts removed if crunchy, soaked in water or milk for 5 minutes, then liquid squeezed out

1 teaspoon **tomato paste**

½ teaspoon **dried oregano**

½ teaspoon **ground cumin**

½ teaspoon **ground coriander**

½ teaspoon **paprika** (optional)

a generous pinch of **sumac** (optional)

½–1 teaspoon **dried red pepper flakes**

1 teaspoon chopped **fresh dill** or

⅛ teaspoon **dried dill**

1 tablespoon finely chopped **fresh parsley**

salt and **freshly ground black pepper**

TO SERVE:

your choice of a smear of **harissa** or **hamburger relish**, **Pink Pickled Onions** (see page 185), crumbled **feta cheese**, **Tzatziki** (see page 194), **cucumber**, finely sliced diced **tomatoes**, or crisp **lettuce**

4 **burger buns**, sliced in half and warmed or toasted

Pour a splash of oil into a wide skillet set over medium heat. When hot, add the onion and a pinch of salt and cook, stirring often, for 6–8 minutes, or until the onion is just beginning to soften. Add the garlic and cook for another minute.

Transfer the lamb to a large bowl and add the onion and garlic. Crumble the bread into the bowl. Add the tomato paste, oregano, ground spices, dried red flakes, dill, parsley, ½ teaspoon of salt, and a liberal dusting of black pepper. Mix everything together well, but don't be too vigorous or the burgers will lose their meaty texture.

Wipe out the skillet and add a little more oil, swirling it about to coat the bottom. Put over medium heat to warm up. Fry a little nugget of the burger mix until cooked through. Taste and add more seasoning, herbs, or dried red pepper flakes, if needed. Divide the lamb mixture into four, then shape into patties, each about ¾ inch thick and about 4 inches across. Cook for about 4 minutes, or until the bottoms of the patties are thoroughly browned. (Try not to move the patties around too much, and don't press them with a spatula, because this squeezes out their delicious juices.)

Gently turn the patties over. Cook for another 4 minutes or until the patties are dark brown on the bottom and just cooked through. If possible, let the patties rest, out of the pan, for a couple of minutes before serving.

Assemble the burgers, bottom bun half first, then whichever combo of garnishes you like, in this order: harissa and/or relish, pickled onions, patty, feta and/or tzatziki, cucumber, tomato, top bun half. Eat immediately.

=TIP=

You can make the patties
and freeze them raw,
separated by pieces
of wax paper. Defrost
them thoroughly
before cooking.

LEON'S CHICKEN BURGER

SERVES 4

PREP TIME: 5 MIN * COOK TIME: 15 MIN

DF | NF | SoF

neutral cooking oil

4 boneless **chicken thighs**

4 **burger buns**, sliced in half and warmed
    or toasted

LEON Tarragon Mayo (see page 188)

12 slices of fresh **cucumber** or sliced
    Dill Pickles (see page 185)

1 **beefsteak tomato**, sliced into 4 rounds

a big handful of **arugula**

salt and **freshly ground black pepper**

your favorite sides, to serve

If you love our grilled chicken burger, we hope you will love this version, too. To change things a little, head to pages 196–97, where we've collected our favorite meaty rubs, and then look at pages 188–95, where you'll find sauces that complement each one.

Remove the skin from the chicken, if you like. Put a wide skillet over medium heat and add a splash of oil. Season the thighs generously all over with salt and pepper. If they are thick, make a few deep cuts into the thicker parts with a sharp knife to help speed up the cooking. Put the meat into the hot pan. Cook, turning often, for up to 15 minutes, until browned all over and cooked through. Check by piercing a thick piece, the meat should be cooked through—with no pink remaining—and the juices should run clear. Cover the pan with a lid to hurry things along, if necessary, but don't let the meat burn.

Lay out the burger buns in front of you. Place a dollop of tarragon mayo on each half, then place three slices of cucumber or dill pickles on the bottom bun halves, then a slice of tomato, then some arugula. Place the chicken on top, then finish with the tops of the buns.

Eat immediately, with your favorite sides.

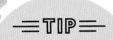

=TIP=

The Avocado and Butter Lettuce salad (see page 87) is the perfect side for this burger.

BEET, CARROT & ONION BHAJI BURGERS

SERVES 4

PREP TIME: 25 MIN * COOK TIME: 20 MIN

V | NF | SoF

vegetable oil

1 teaspoon **mustard seeds**

1 teaspoon **cumin seeds**

4 **curry leaves**, crumbled

1 large **onion**, very finely sliced

2 small **carrots** (about 3½ oz), peeled and finely sliced into thin matchsticks

1 medium **beet**, peeled and finely sliced into thin matchsticks

2 tablespoons finely chopped **fresh cilantro leaves**

1 teaspoon finely chopped, seeded **red** or **green chili**

½ teaspoon **black cumin (nigella) seeds**

2 teaspoons **freshly squeezed lime juice**

1 teaspoon **ground turmeric**

1⅔ cups **chickpea (besan) flour**

2½ tablespoons **rice flour**

½ teaspoon **baking powder**

salt and **freshly ground black pepper**

TO SERVE:

8 **mini naan**, or cut up a **large naan** or 8 **burger buns**

Indian pickles or **chutney**

½ cup **Garlicky Yogurt** (see page 194; optional)

thinly sliced **cucumber**

pomegranate seeds

These are insane. A rainbow of good-for-you vegetables in a delicious chickpea batter, spiked with chili and black cumin seeds. Be sure to get really good-quality, fresh fluffy naan. If you can't get good ones, use regular burger buns.

Pour a tablespoon of oil into a small saucepan over medium heat and add the mustard seeds. When they start to pop, add the cumin seeds and curry leaves. Cook for 1 minute, making sure the cumin doesn't burn. Remove from the heat and scrape the pan out into a large bowl. Add the onion, carrots, beet, cilantro, chili, black cumin seeds, lime juice, turmeric, and a generous pinch of salt and pepper.

Stir together the flours and baking powder. Add to the bowl and then slowly add up to ¾ cup of cold water, stirring all the time, until everything is coated in a smooth batter about the thickness of light cream.

Heat about ½ inch of vegetable oil in a wide skillet set over medium heat. Line a plate with paper towels. Place the naan or burger buns in a low oven to warm up. Have ready all the pickles/chutneys and garnishes, plus garlicky yogurt, if using.

Use a large spoon to scoop a little of the patty mixture into the pan. Cook until golden, turning once, then lift out carefully using tongs. Cool a little, then taste and add more seasoning to the batter, if needed. When happy, use the spoon to make a bhaji burger about 3¼ inches across and ½ inch thick. Cook two or three at a time for 3–4 minutes, until they turn a deep golden. (Keep an eye on how hot the oil is— if you use a candy thermometer, 350°F is ideal). Then turn and repeat. Remove from the pan and drain on the lined plate. Keep warm while you cook the rest.

Assemble the mini naan burgers quickly (two per person) and eat immediately.

=TIP=

If freezing the cooked patties, defrost thoroughly before reheating, then microwave on high for 1½ minutes per patty, until hot throughout. Crisp up briefly in a skillet (you won't need more oil).

STUFFED MUSHROOM BURGERS

SERVES 4

PREP TIME: 10 MIN * COOK TIME: 35–45 MIN

V | SoF

4 large **portobello mushrooms**

3 tablespoons **extra virgin olive oil**,
plus extra for serving

5 large sprigs of **fresh thyme**, leaves picked

zest and juice of ½ **unwaxed lemon**

3 cloves of **garlic**, peeled

2 tablespoons **olive oil**

3 tablespoons **pine nuts**

1 lb **baby spinach leaves**

7 oz **rinded goat cheese log**, sliced into
4 thick disks

4 good-quality **burger buns**, sliced in half
and warmed or toasted

a small bunch of **fresh basil**, leaves picked

salt and **freshly ground black pepper**

=TIP=

Make sure the
mushrooms are a good
size, at least as big as
your palm.

These burgers are meaty, tangy, and juicy (and you won't miss the beef). They are a little tricky to prepare but are definitely worth it.

Heat the oven to 400°F.

Cut the stems off the mushrooms and discard, then place the mushrooms on a baking pan, gill side up. Drizzle the mushrooms with the extra virgin olive oil, then sprinkle with the thyme leaves, some salt and pepper, and a pinch of the lemon zest.

Bake for about 20 minutes, then flip over, spoon over any juices, and bake for another 10–15 minutes, until the mushrooms have roasted, shriveled, softened, and intensified in flavor. Remove from the oven and set aside.

While the mushrooms are in the oven, prepare the spinach and pine nut filling.

Put a skillet over medium heat. While it is coming up to temperature, finely slice the garlic. Add the olive oil to the pan and fry the pine nuts for a few minutes until fragrant. Add the garlic and fry briefly for about 1 minute. Finally, add the spinach and fry until wilted—not more than a couple of minutes. Season with salt and pepper and a splash of lemon juice to wake up the flavors. Set aside.

Divide the spinach-and-pine nut mixture among the mushrooms (let any excess liquid drain back into the pan) and top each with a slice of goat cheese. Return to the oven for 5–10 minutes or until the cheese melts and bubbles.

To serve, place one stuffed mushroom in each burger bun, topping with a drizzle of extra virgin olive oil, a pinch each of salt and the remaining lemon zest, and the freshly torn basil leaves. Eat immediately.

STEAK BURRITO

SERVES 2
PREP TIME: 15 MIN * COOK TIME: 18 MIN
NF | SoF

¼ cup **long-grain** or **basmati rice**

¼ teaspoon **ground cumin**

¼ teaspoon **dried oregano**

⅛ teaspoon **cayenne pepper**

½ clove of **garlic**, crushed

juice of ½ **lime**

7 oz **skirt steak**, fat trimmed away

neutral cooking oil

salt and **freshly ground black pepper**

FOR THE BURRITOS:

2 large **wraps/flatbreads**, warm

⅔ cup cooked **black beans**, hot or warm

3 tablespoons **feta cheese** (ideally a mild one)

¼ cup **Guacamole** (see page 195), or 1 **avocado**, peeled, pitted, and mashed (optional)

½ **scallion**, sliced, or about 1 tablespoon **Pink Pickled Onions** (see page 185), or both

pickled jalapeños, sliced or chopped

4 **cherry tomatoes**, finely chopped

a handful of **fresh cilantro leaves**

Hot sauce, to taste

Many burritos are made with wonderfully tasty slow-cooked meats, which goes against this book's speedy ethos. So we invented a reverse-engineered way to max out flavor by flash-cooking skirt steak—an especially tasty cut—until rare and tender, then dressing it with lime and garlic as it rests. (You could treat cooked chicken or fish in the same way, or swap the steak for fried chorizo, or alternatively make this vegetarian by using the black beans on page 60.)

Put the rice with ½ cup of water into a saucepan. Bring to a boil, then cover and cook for about 12 minutes, or according to package directions, until tender. Remove from the heat, drain if necessary, and set aside (covered) while you prepare the rest of the fillings.

Mix together the cumin, oregano, cayenne pepper, garlic, lime juice, and some salt and pepper in a small bowl. Set aside.

Season the steak all over. Pour a little oil into a skillet set over high heat. When it's really hot, quickly cook the steak just 2–3 minutes on each side, until deep brown on both sides but still fairly rare. Remove from the pan and place in a bowl. Pour over the lime juice mixture and set aside to rest.

When ready to assemble, slice the steak into ½-inch-thick strips. Arrange half the rice in a line on each wrap/flatbread, leaving space at the bottom to fold up and enclose the fillings later. Divide the black beans, feta, steak strips, and guacamole or avocado, if using, between the wraps. Arrange all the remaining vegetables and cilantro leaves on top. Douse everything generously with hot sauce, then tightly wrap up each burrito, tucking up the spare wrap/flatbread at the bottom before rolling from the side, so that the filling doesn't fall out or drip. Dig in.

FALAFEL & HARISSA WRAPS

SERVES 4

PREP TIME: 15 MIN * COOK TIME: 25 MIN

V | NF | SoF

FOR THE FALAFEL:

1½ cups drained and rinsed **canned chickpeas (garbanzo beans)**

1 small **onion**, coarsely chopped

2 cloves of **garlic**, coarsely chopped

½ teaspoon **fine salt**

1 teaspoon **ground cumin**

1 teaspoon **ground coriander**

a pinch of **cayenne pepper**

generous pinch of **ground cinnamon**

dusting of **freshly ground black pepper**

1 teaspoon **freshly squeezed lemon juice**

1 teaspoon **baking powder**

2 teaspoons **all-purpose flour**

⅓ cup **chickpea (besan) flour**

olive oil

TO SERVE:

4 **flatbreads/wraps**, warmed

harissa

Tahini Sauce (see page 29)

crisp lettuce leaves, slices of **cucumber**, **pickled green chilies**

optional extras: crumbled **feta cheese** or strips of fried **halloumi**, **Tzatziki** (see page 194), **Pickled Radishes** (see page 185), **Pink Pickled Onions** (see page 185), or finely sliced **scallions**

Traditionally, chickpea falafel are deep-fried, which makes them very crisp. These are pan-fried, so they're both easier to cook and richer in texture, making them perfect for wrapping in flatbreads. (LEON's restaurant falafel are made with sweet potato and baked, so these are a little different.)

For the falafel, put the chickpeas, onion, garlic, salt, cumin, coriander, cayenne pepper, cinnamon, black pepper, and lemon juice into a food processor and pulse until you have a thick, coarse paste. Transfer the mixture to a bowl, add the baking powder and both flours, and stir well to combine. The batter should be scoopable but not sloppy. If it seems wet, add another 1–2 tablespoons of chickpea flour.

Set a large skillet over medium heat and add about ¼ inch of olive oil. When shimmering hot, add a little of the falafel batter to the pan and cook for 2 minutes, turning, then cool and taste. Add salt or more of any other flavorings to taste.

When ready to cook, use a soup spoon to form 3–4 falafel portions. Add to the pan and flatten them into patties, each about 3¼ inches across. Cook gently for about 4 minutes or until deep golden brown—reduce the heat if they cook too fast. Gently flip each one over and cook for 3–4 minutes, until both sides are crisp. Remove from the pan and drain on a plate lined with paper towels while you cook the rest in the same way, adding more oil as needed (making about 12 falafel in total).

To assemble, lay out the flatbreads/wraps and place three falafel on each one, leaving some room at the bottom to turn up the wrap later. Drizzle over some harissa and tahini sauce, making sure it hits each falafel. Arrange the lettuce, cucumber, and pickled chilies next to the falafel, and add any extra fillings, if using. Turn the bottom of each wrap up to enclose, then roll the sides inward. Scoff immediately.

≡TIP≡

You can, of course, use store-bought falafel here, but first warm them before you assemble the wraps.

SABICH

SERVES 4

PREP TIME: 30 MIN * COOK TIME: 10–15 MIN

DF | V | NF | SoF

Sabich is an incredibly popular Israeli street food. It was introduced by Iraqi Jews who, on the Sabbath, when no cooking was allowed, ate prefried eggplant slices, hard-boiled eggs, and pita bread. This modern formulation is an unusual combination of flavors, but it really works.

FOR THE SALAD:

3 **plum tomatoes**, cored and diced

½ large **cucumber**, diced

1 small **red onion**, thinly sliced

a handful of **fresh parsley**, coarsely chopped

2 tablespoons **olive oil**

juice of ½ **lemon**

½ teaspoon each **ground cumin** and **sumac**

salt and **freshly ground black pepper**

FOR THE CABBAGE:

½ head of **red cabbage**, shredded

2 tablespoons **red wine vinegar**

FOR THE TAHINI SAUCE:

2 cloves of **garlic**, crushed

2 tablespoons **freshly squeezed lemon juice**

¼ cup **tahini**

¼ teaspoon **ground cumin**

FOR THE EGGPLANT:

3 tablespoons **vegetable oil**

1 **large eggplant**, in ½-inch-thick disks

salt

TO SERVE:

4 **pita breads**

½ cup any **Hummus** (see pages 186–87)

4 hard-boiled **eggs**, cooled, peeled, sliced

¼ cup good-quality **mango chutney**

Combine all the salad ingredients in a bowl, mix thoroughly, and check the seasoning.

Combine the cabbage ingredients in a bowl with ½ teaspoon of salt.

For the tahini sauce, first blend the garlic and lemon juice together in a small food processor to remove some of the harshness from the garlic. Then add the tahini, cumin, and 2 tablespoons of cold water and blend until smooth and drizzle-able, adding more water if too thick. Season with salt to taste.

When ready to cook the eggplant, heat the vegetable oil in a large skillet over medium-high heat until shimmering. Fry the eggplant for about 5 minutes on each side, turning once, until golden brown and tender. Place on a tray lined with paper towels and sprinkle with a little salt.

Wipe out the pan, return to the heat, and toast the pita breads for 30 seconds on each side. Slit a little pocket in the top of each. Smear 2 tablespoons of hummus inside each pita, stuff in 3–4 fried eggplant slices and one sliced egg, top with the salad and cabbage, dollop on a tablespoon of mango chutney and drizzle with as much tahini sauce as you want.

Eat immediately, served with plenty of napkins.

CHICKEN SHAWARMA

SERVES 4

PREP TIME: 20 MIN, PLUS MARINATING * COOK TIME: 20 MIN

DF | NF | SoF

FOR THE CHICKEN MARINADE:

1 teaspoon **garlic powder** or **granules**

½ teaspoon **ground turmeric**

½ teaspoon **ground cumin**

½ teaspoon **ground coriander**

¼ teaspoon **ground cinnamon**

a pinch of **ground allspice**

½ teaspoon **sumac** (optional)

¼ teaspoon **cayenne pepper**

juice of ½ **lemon**

1 teaspoon **paprika**

1 tablespoon **olive** or **vegetable oil**, plus
   extra for cooking

½ teaspoon **fine salt**

1¼ lb skin-on, boneless **chicken thighs**

TO SERVE:

1 small clove of **garlic**, crushed to a paste

1–2 teaspoons **freshly squeezed lemon juice**

1 tablespoon **tahini**

a generous pinch of **salt**

4 **flatbreads** or **pita breads**

garnishes: your choice of **crisp lettuce**,
   Pink Pickled Onions (see page 185), or
   finely sliced **red onion, pickled green
   chilies**, finely diced to**matoes**, chopped
   fresh parsley

hot sauce or **harissa**

This is our pan-cooked version of a late-night, takeout classic. You can serve it with Garlicky Yogurt (see page 194) instead of tahini, if you prefer, or use the Tzatziki on page 194. Turkey or lamb would also work in this recipe.

Mix together all the marinade ingredients, except the chicken, in a large bowl. If the chicken pieces are chunky, make a few small cuts to open up the meat, or cut the thighs into smaller pieces to help speed up the cooking process later. Add the chicken to the bowl and massage the marinade into the meat. Cover and refrigerate for as long as possible—15 minutes is fine, but an hour or more would be better.

Just before you are ready to cook, mix together the garlic, 1 teaspoon of the lemon juice, the tahini, and pinch of salt. Stir until smooth, adding a little water if necessary, until you have a pourable sauce. Taste and add more lemon or salt, if needed.

When ready to cook, add a splash of oil to a wide skillet set over low-medium heat. Add the chicken and cook gently, making sure it cooks through evenly without burning, for 15–17 minutes, turning once or twice. When the chicken is cooked through (check a thick piece to see if the meat is done and the juices run clear), set the pan aside and let rest. Meanwhile, warm or toast the flatbreads either under a broiler or better, over a gas ring, using tongs. Pita breads are best toasted under the broiler or in the toaster.

Transfer the chicken to a board and thinly slice, cutting diagonally across the grain of the meat. Save any juices and add to those in the pan. Arrange the meat with your chosen garnishes on the warm flatbreads. Drizzle with the tahini sauce, hot sauce or harissa, and some of the pan juices—but don't make it too wet. Wrap up, tucking the bread in at the bottom to prevent drips, and eat immediately.

GOZLEME

2 cups **all-purpose flour**, plus extra for dusting
⅓ cup **plain yogurt**
olive oil, for cooking and brushing
1 **zucchini**, shredded
1⅓ cups crumbled **feta cheese**
4 oz **halloumi**, finely diced (or extra **feta**)
a pinch of **mild dried red pepper flakes**
2 **scallions**, minced
2 tablespoons finely chopped **fresh dill**
3 tablespoons finely chopped **fresh parsley**
10 **fresh mint leaves**, finely chopped
salt and **freshly ground black pepper**

Although this is a quick version of a popular Turkish stuffed flatbread, you could make it even quicker by using store-bought flatbreads. Place one in a hot, dry pan, cover one half with the filling, then fold over to enclose. Cook for a couple of minutes until the bottom is golden, then flip and cook the other side.

Mix the flour and 1 teaspoon of salt in a large mixing bowl. Whisk the yogurt with scant ½ cup of water, then gradually mix it into the flour, using only as much as you need to make a soft, but not sticky, dough. Knead on a clean, floured surface for a couple f minutes. Then set aside to rest.

Pour a splash of oil into a large skillet set over low-medium heat. Add a tiny pinch of salt to the zucchini and spread thinly across the pan to remove moisture from the zucchini without browning it. Cook, stirring occasionally, for about 5 minutes. Remove the pan from the heat.

Meanwhile, mix together the remaining ingredients. When the zucchini is cooked, add it to this mixture, along with a good dose of black pepper.

Divide the dough into eight equal pieces and shape into balls. Flour your work surface and a rolling pin. Wipe out the skillet and return to low heat.

Roll out one of the balls as thinly as possible to a 10-inch disk, until almost translucent. Keep dusting with flour and turning the pastry so it doesn't stick.

Evenly spread about 2 tablespoons of the filling across half of the disk, then fold over to form a semicircle. Press the edges together, then trim away the excess dough, making sure the two layers remain sealed. Brush the top with olive oil and place, oiled side down, into the hot pan. Cook for 4–5 minutes, until little brown dots appear all over the bottom. Brush the top with oil, then flip over and cook the other side. The gozleme is cooked when both sides are covered in golden brown dots, and you can't see any raw dough (you may need to flip it again, and press sections of the dough onto the pan, to make sure it is all cooked). Repeat to assemble and cook the other gozlemes, keeping the cooked ones warm on a plate or wrapped in a clean dish towel.

Serve the gozleme immediately, cut into wedges or strips.

PANEER & BEET WRAP

SERVES 4

PREP TIME: 20 MIN * COOK TIME: 10–15 MIN

V | NF | SoF

FOR THE PANEER:
⅓ cup **vegetable oil**
1 teaspoon **ground turmeric**
1 teaspoon **ground cumin**
1 teaspoon **ground coriander**
1 teaspoon **garlic powder**
1 teaspoon **garam masala**
1 teaspoon **smoked paprika**
½ teaspoon **cayenne pepper**
1 lb **paneer**, cut into ½-inch cubes
salt and **freshly ground black pepper**

FOR THE BEET PUREE:
6 **cooked beets** (not in vinegar)
½ cup shredded **dry unsweetened coconut**
1 tablespoon **olive oil**
salt

FOR THE CURRY YOGURT:
1 cup **Greek yogurt**
2 teaspoons **mild curry powder**
freshly squeezed lime juice, to taste
salt and **freshly ground black pepper**

TO SERVE:
4 **naan**s, warm
3 tablespoons **Pink Pickled Onions** (see page 185) or finely sliced **red onion**
a big handful of **fresh cilantro leaves**
1 **lime**, cut into wedges

Jack's dad hates cheese. "What's paneer?," he demanded as Jack put this down in front of him. "It's kind of like an Indian halloumi . . ." "No. Absolutely not," he barked. "Just try it. Please." Well, he loved it. And you will, too.

For the paneer, in a large bowl, mix together ¼ cup of the vegetable oil and all the spices and seasonings with ½ teaspoon each of salt and pepper. Add the paneer and mix thoroughly, making sure each piece is well coated. Set aside.

For the beet puree, put the beets and a splash of water into a food processor and blend until smooth. Add a splash more water, if necessary. Taste for seasoning and adjust with salt. Lightly toast the coconut in a dry skillet over low heat, stirring often, until light golden. Add to the beets, along with the oil, and pulse to combine. Set aside.

To make the curry yogurt, whisk together all the ingredients in a bowl. Taste for seasoning and lime, and adjust if needed.

Heat the remaining 2 tablespoons of vegetable oil in a large skillet over medium heat. When it is shimmering, add the spice-coated paneer cubes and fry for 3–4 minutes, until golden brown, then flip over and fry the other side for another 2–3 minutes, until golden brown.

To serve, smear a generous amount of beet puree on each naan, then top with the paneer cubes. Drizzle with some curry yogurt and top with a generous amount of onions and cilantro leaves. Serve with lime wedges on the side.

LAMB SOUVLAKI WITH TZATZIKI

SERVES 6

PREP TIME: 15 MIN, PLUS MARINATING * COOK TIME: 8–12 MIN

NF | SoF

FOR THE LAMB:
⅓ cup **extra virgin olive oil**

zest and juice of 1 **unwaxed lemon**

3 large cloves of **garlic**, crushed

1½ teaspoons **salt**

10 twists of **freshly ground black pepper**

1 teaspoon **dried oregano**

1 teaspoon **ground cumin**

2 sprigs of **fresh rosemary**, leaves picked and finely chopped

2¼ lb **lamb shoulder**, trimmed of any fat and cut into 1¼-inch cubes

1 large **red onion**, chopped into 1¼-inch wedges

1 large **red bell pepper**, seeded and chopped into 1¼-inch squares

6–12 **metal skewers** (or if using wooden/bamboo skewers, soak them in water for 20 minutes before use)

vegetable oil, for greasing

TO SERVE:
a small bunch of **fresh parsley leaves**

6 **pita breads**

Tzatziki (see page 194)

Here is a Greek-style skewer and hugely popular street food dish. It is usually made with meat, but you can make it vegetarian by threading the kabobs with chunks of halloumi instead.

In a large mixing bowl, whisk together the olive oil, lemon zest and juice, garlic, salt, pepper, oregano, cumin, and chopped rosemary. Add the lamb cubes and mix thoroughly, making sure every cube is coated. Cover and refrigerate for at least 4 hours, but preferably overnight.

To assemble the skewers, thread alternating pieces of lamb, red onion, and red bell pepper onto the skewers until each skewer is full.

Heat a barbecue grill or broiler to high heat. Oil the grates or rack with vegetable oil. Cook the skewers, basting with the remaining marinade, for 2–3 minutes on each side, until golden and charred on the outside and light pink in the middle, cooking them for 8–12 minutes in total.

Just before you're ready to serve, toast the pita breads for a few minutes in a dry skillet. Transfer the skewers to serving plates, sprinkle with the parsley leaves, and serve each portion with a generous dollop of tzatziki and a pita bread alongside.

HARISSA CHICKEN KABOBS
WITH HERBED YOGURT & POMEGRANATE

SERVES 4

PREP TIME: 15 MIN, PLUS MARINATING ＊ COOK TIME: 10–15 MIN

SoF

FOR THE CHICKEN:

4 large skinless, boneless **chicken breasts**

¼ cup **harissa**

1 teaspoon **ground cumin**

1 teaspoon **salt**

1 teaspoon **freshly ground black pepper**

a splash of **olive oil**, if needed

4 **metal skewers**

2 tablespoons **vegetable oil**

FOR THE YOGURT:

1 cup **Greek yogurt**

1 clove of **garlic**, grated

zest and juice of ½ **unwaxed lemon**

a small bunch of **fresh basil leaves**, finely chopped

a small bunch of **fresh mint leaves**, finely chopped

salt and **freshly ground black pepper**

TO SERVE:

2 **lemons**

4 **flatbreads** (**khobez** or **naans** work really well), warmed

a handful of **toasted pine nuts**

a handful of **pomegranate seeds**

Jack grew up in Haringey, North London, where there is an abundance of Greek and Turkish kabob takeouts (if you're in the area, E. Mono in Kentish Town is the undisputed king of kabobs). This is his version of a favorite childhood dish.

Cut the chicken into 1¼-inch cubes, put into a large mixing bowl, and rub with the harissa, cumin, salt, and pepper. Add a splash of olive oil if the mix is a little sticky. Cover and let marinate in the refrigerator for at least an hour (4–6 hours would be ideal).

Put the yogurt, grated garlic, lemon zest and juice, basil, and mint into a bowl and mix well until everything is combined. Season with a little salt and pepper. Cover and set aside.

Thread the chicken pieces evenly onto the skewers. Heat the vegetable oil in a ridged grill pan over medium-high heat. When hot, place the skewers in the pan and grill for about 5 minutes, until a golden char appears on the bottom. Resist the temptation to keep turning them. Turn over with some tongs and grill on the other side until the meat is completely cooked. Transfer to a plate while you grill the lemons.

Cut the lemons in half and remove any visible seeds with the tip of your knife. Put the lemons, cut side down, into the same pan in which you cooked the chicken and cook for 3–4 minutes or until a brown crust appears on the cut sides. Set aside.

To assemble the wraps, place a flatbread in the palm of your hand and use it to pull the chicken off one skewer. Smear on some yogurt, sprinkle with some pine nuts and pomegranate seeds, and serve each with a charred lemon half for squeezing.

SPICED CAULIFLOWER NAAN

SERVES 4

PREP TIME: 20 MIN * COOK TIME: 15–20 MIN

V | SoF

FOR THE CAULIFLOWER:
1 large **cauliflower**
3 tablespoons **extra virgin olive oil**
2 teaspoons **ground cumin**
1 teaspoon **ground turmeric**
½ teaspoon **medium chili powder**
salt and **freshly ground black pepper**

FOR THE MINT YOGURT:
1 cup **Greek yogurt**
a handful of **fresh mint leaves**, finely
    chopped
1 clove of **garlic**, grated
zest and juice of ½ **unwaxed lemon**
salt and **freshly ground black pepper**

FOR THE HAZELNUT SAUCE:
⅔ cup **blanched hazelnuts**
⅓ cup freshly grated **Parmesan cheese** (or
    use **vegetarian Parmesan-style cheese**)
juice of ½ **lemon**
2 tablespoons **extra virgin olive oil**, plus
    extra if the sauce is a little thick
salt and **freshly ground black pepper**

TO SERVE:
4 **naans**, warm
a big handful of **pomegranate seeds**
a big handful of **fresh cilantro leaves**
about ¼ cup **Pink Pickled Onions** (see
    page 185)

This is a delicious wrap inspired by the one Jack and Rebecca shared at Flank in Victoria when we were initially planning the book. The spiciness of the cauliflower is offset wonderfully by the nutty sauce and yogurt. You can also serve this without the naan as a warm salad, with a few big handfuls of watercress dressed with lemon juice and olive oil.

Heat the oven to 425°F.

Cut the cauliflower into small florets. Put into a roasting pan and drizzle with the olive oil. Sprinkle with the spices, some salt, and a few twists of black pepper and toss well to combine. Roast for 15–20 minutes or until browned.

While the cauliflower is in the oven, make the mint yogurt. Combine all the ingredients in a bowl and season to taste.

Next, make the hazelnut sauce. Toast the hazelnuts in a dry skillet for a few minutes until fragrant and light golden. Let cool, then, in a food processor, process together the hazelnuts, Parmesan, and lemon juice with 2 tablespoons of water. Slowly drizzle in the oil with the blades running until you get the consistency you want. It should look more like a hummus than a pesto. Taste for seasoning and acidity, adjust if necessary, then process one last time.

Now assemble the wraps. Spoon a generous amount of hazelnut sauce into the middle of each naan and smear evenly lengthwise. Top with some roasted cauliflower and mint yogurt, then sprinkle with some pomegranate seeds, cilantro leaves, and pink pickled onions. Serve immediately.

CAJUN-STYLE FISH WRAP WITH SLAW

SERVES 4

PREP TIME: 10 MIN ✳ COOK TIME: 10–15 MIN

NF | SoF

FOR THE FISH:

2 teaspoons **salt**

2 teaspoons **freshly ground black pepper**

2 teaspoons **paprika**

2 teaspoons **smoked paprika**

2 teaspoons **cayenne pepper**

2 teaspoons **garlic powder**

2 teaspoons **onion powder**

2 teaspoons **dried oregano**

2 teaspoons **dried thyme**

4 tablespoons **butter**

4 small firm **white fish fillets**, such as **halibut**, **cod**, or **flounder**

1 tablespoon **vegetable oil**

1 **lime**, cut into wedges

TO SERVE:

4 **tortilla wraps**, warm

4 big spoonfuls of **slaw** (either **Classic Coleslaw**, see page 95, or **Grazka's Fennel Slaw**, see page 96)

1 large ripe **avocado**, peeled, pitted, and thinly sliced

extra virgin olive oil, for drizzling

1 **lime**, cut into wedges

a few sprigs of **dill**, coarsely chopped (optional)

salt

Blackened fish is a Cajun favorite. It is traditionally made with grouper rolled in the distinctive Cajun seasoning, then "blackened" in a pan. We've put it in a wrap, served with creamy avocado and a tangy slaw. If you can't find grouper, use other white fish.

For the fish, mix the salt, spices, garlic and onion powders, and herbs together in a bowl, then place on a plate.

Add 3 tablespoons of the butter to a large, heavy skillet and gently melt, then pour it into a shallow bowl.

Dip each fish fillet in the melted butter, then dredge in the spice mix.

Place the same skillet back over medium-high heat and add the oil. When it is shimmering, place the fillets in, one by one, laying them away from you to avoid being splashed by hot oil. Cook for 3–4 minutes until browned. Turn the fish, add the remaining butter, breaking it up and placing it in various spots around the pan, and cook for another 3–4 minutes, until the other side is brown and the fish flakes easily. Transfer the fillets to a plate and squeeze a little lime juice over each one.

To assemble the wraps, place a layer of slaw on each wrap, followed by a fish fillet, then top with avocado slices, a drizzle of extra virgin olive oil, and a pinch of salt. Serve each with lime wedges on the side and sprinkled with dill, if you want.

TIP

If you are short on time, you can buy store-bought Cajun seasoning. But we like to make a big batch of our own and store it in an airtight container for future use (see page 196).

✳ASIAN FISH STICK WRAP

SERVES 4

PREP TIME: 20 MIN ✳ COOK TIME: 10 MIN

DF | NF

FOR THE SLAW:

3 tablespoons **rice vinegar**

2 tablespoons **soy sauce**

2 tablespoons **honey**

1 tablespoon **sesame oil**

1 teaspoon minced **fresh ginger**

1 teaspoon minced **garlic**

½ head of **red cabbage**, thinly sliced

2 medium or 1 large **carrot**, cut into
matchsticks

2 **scallions**, thinly sliced

2 **radishes**, thinly sliced

FOR THE FISH:

⅔ cup **all-purpose flour**

2 **eggs**, beaten

2 cups **panko bread crumbs**

4 small **white fish fillets** (**cod**, **halibut**,
Alaskan pollock, **red snapper**), cut into
fish stick-size rectangles

3 tablespoons **vegetable oil**

salt and **freshly ground black pepper**

TO SERVE:

4 **tortilla wraps**, warm

1 **avocado**, peeled, pitted, and thinly sliced

Sriracha Mayo (see page 188)

1 **lime**, cut into wedges

flaky sea salt and **freshly ground black
pepper**, to taste

*A fresh take on the fish stick sandwich and one to try if you like LEON's fish stick
wrap. Crispy breaded fish with a spicy Sriracha mayo and tangy slaw.*

For the slaw, in a large bowl, whisk together the rice vinegar, soy sauce, honey,
sesame oil, ginger, and garlic to make the dressing.

Add the red cabbage, carrot, scallions, and radishes. Mix thoroughly and let
marinate while you prepare and cook the fish.

Put the flour, beaten eggs, and panko bread crumbs into three separate shallow
bowls. Season each fish stick with a pinch of salt and pepper, then place in the flour
bowl and coat thoroughly, dusting off any excess. Do the same with the egg, then
the same with the bread crumbs. Place on a tray and repeat until all the fish sticks
are coated.

Heat the oil in a large skillet over medium heat. When shimmering, add the fish
sticks and fry for 3–4 minutes, until golden brown on the underside. Flip and repeat,
frying for another 3–4 minutes, until the other side is golden brown. Transfer to a
plate lined with paper towels to drain off any excess oil.

To assemble each wrap, place a handful of slaw on a tortilla wrap, top with a quarter
of the fish sticks and avocado slices, spoon over some Sriracha mayo, squeeze with a
lime wedge, season to taste, then roll up and eat.

CRAB & FENNEL SANDWICH

SERVES 2

PREP TIME: 5 MIN

NF | SoF

4 slices of good-quality **bread** (sourdough is good here, or good-quality white bread), or **brioche**

about 3 tablespoons good-quality **mayonnaise**

3½ oz fresh **white crabmeat**, or a mixture of **white and brown crabmeat**

15 very thin slices of **cucumber**

¼ **fennel** bulb, finely sliced

freshly squeezed lemon juice, to taste

freshly ground black pepper

This takes us back to sunny vacations on the beach along the British coast.

If your bread is soft, it's a good idea to lightly toast it before building the sandwich.

Spread the bread slices lightly with the mayonnaise, then top two slices with the cucumber and fennel and squeeze some lemon juice over them. Divide the crabmeat between the two slices, season with plenty of black pepper (you probably won't need any salt), then top with the remaining slices of bread.

Eat immediately.

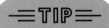

TIP

We like to keep the crab and mayo separate, but if you prefer, you can mix them together before spreading over the bread.

SMOKED MACKEREL SANDWICH
WITH PICKLES & CHIVES

SERVES 2

PREP TIME: 5 MIN

DF | NF | SoF

4 large slices of **crusty bread** (ideally good **sourdough**)

about 1 tablespoon good-quality **mayonnaise**

2 good-quality skinless **smoked mackerel fillets**, torn into 1¼–1½-inch pieces

1 teaspoon finely chopped **fresh chives**

thinly sliced **Dill Pickles** (see page 185) or **pickles** from a jar

about 20 thin slices of **cucumber**

freshly squeezed lemon juice, to taste

freshly ground black pepper

Mackerel is good for you and it's rich in heart-healthy fats that most of us don't get enough of. But more to the point, smoked and paired with pickles, it tastes amazing. This is also great with ribbons of very thinly sliced fennel.

You need the bread to have some crunch, otherwise this sandwich can feel squishy, so toast it lightly if necessary.

Check how dry or oily the mackerel is. If it's fatty, be sparing with the mayo, but if it's on the dry side, you can be more generous. Spread two of the bread slices with mayo. Top with the sliced cucumber—you need a lot, because it's the only thing giving the sandwich crispy texture. Next, arrange the pickles, chives, and mackerel on top. Squeeze a little lemon juice over it and dust the whole assembly with plenty of black pepper.

Top with the remaining slices of bread and eat immediately (standing at the kitchen counter, if you're anything like us).

BAKED MEATBALL SUB

SERVES 4 (WITH A FEW MEATBALLS LEFT OVER FOR THE FREEZER)
PREP TIME: 15 MIN * COOK TIME: 20 MIN
NF | SoF

1 lb good-quality **ground beef**

1 **scallion**, minced

2 cloves of **garlic**, crushed

1 tablespoon freshly grated **Parmesan cheese**, plus extra to serve

2 tablespoons **fresh bread crumbs**

1 **egg**, beaten

2 sprigs of **fresh basil**, leaves from 1 sprig finely chopped

½ teaspoon **salt**

¾ cup **tomato puree** or **tomato sauce**

a splash of **olive oil**

a pinch of **dried red dried pepper flakes** (optional)

salt and **freshly ground black pepper**

4 **sub rolls** (or any kind of **long, sturdy roll** or **baguette**), sliced in half and warmed, to serve

Whether you call this a sub, hero, hoagie, or something else, this is a true American classic. For a richer version, after assembling the bottom half, top the meatballs with sliced American, mozzarella, provolone, or cheddar cheese and broil until melted.

Heat the oven to 350°F.

Mix together the ground beef, scallion, half the garlic, the Parmesan, bread crumbs, egg, and finely chopped basil, along with the measured salt and plenty of black pepper. Make sure everything is evenly mixed, but don't work the mixture too much or the meatballs will be dense and bouncy when cooked.

Divide the mix into 12 equal amounts and firmly shape each one into a ball, using your hands. Place on a wire rack set inside a baking dish. Bake for 20 minutes, or until cooked, turning the balls once.

Meanwhile, make the sauce. Put the tomato puree or sauce, olive oil, the rest of the garlic, the dried red pepper flakes, if using, and some salt and pepper into a small saucepan and bring to a simmer. Cook for 5 minutes, then remove from the heat and set aside.

When the meatballs are done, set the halved sub rolls out in front of you. Halve the meatballs (or not, if you prefer, but halving stops them from falling out of the sandwich). Spread the cut sides of the bread with a little of the sauce, then stuff with meatballs and pour over a little more sauce. Sprinkle with extra Parmesan and the remaining whole basil leaves, then eat immediately.

BRAGG'S FRIED POINTED CABBAGE SANDWICH

SERVES 4

PREP TIME: 10 MIN ★ COOK TIME: 15 MIN

V

2 tablespoons **olive oil**

2 small or 1 large **pointed cabbage**, halved, cored, and thinly sliced

3 cloves of **garlic**, finely sliced

2–3 tablespoons **Bragg Liquid Aminos spray** (depending on how salty you like things)

4 **naans**, to serve

FOR THE PINE NUT PASTE:

1 cup **pine nuts**

1 clove of **garlic**, grated

juice of ½ **lemon**

1 tablespoon **red wine vinegar**

3 tablespoons **tahini**, well stirred

1 teaspoon **ground cumin**

a pinch of **sumac**

a pinch of **cayenne pepper**

salt and **freshly ground black pepper**

Bragg Liquid Aminos is a glorious ingredient and tastes a little like soy sauce. When fried, it deepens into a warm, sweet, slightly sticky marinade. It pairs perfectly with crispy, garlicky fried pointed (sweetheart) cabbage and plenty of pine nut paste. Serve in a naan or between two slices of white toast. Or try the cabbage as a side dish with a roasted meat.

To make the paste, add all the ingredients, except the salt and pepper, to a food processor. Process everything until smooth (at least 1 full minute). Taste, season, taste again. If the mixture is a little sticky, add a splash of cold water. It should have the consistency of smooth hummus. Process again and set aside.

For the cabbage, heat a large skillet over medium-high heat until hot, then add the oil. Add the cabbage and garlic together (this should stop the garlic from burning during cooking). Add the Bragg Liquid Aminos after a couple of minutes. Taste for seasoning. Add more Bragg if your taste buds tell you to. Toss regularly and fry about 15 minutes, until soft, golden, and crispy on the ends.

Assembly time: Smother each naan with pine nut paste and pile high with crispy cabbage. Roll up and dig in.

LEFTOVER TURKEY SANDWICH
WITH HOMEMADE CRANBERRY SAUCE & BRIE

SERVES 2

PREP TIME: 15 MIN, PLUS COOLING ★ COOK TIME: 15–20 MIN

NF | SoF

FOR THE CRANBERRY SAUCE:

½ cup packed **light brown sugar**

scant ½ cup **freshly squeezed orange juice**

2½ cups **fresh** or **frozen cranberries**

zest of 1 **clementine** or **satsuma**

FOR THE SANDWICH:

1 tablespoon **butter**

2 handfuls of **leftover cooked turkey**

4 slices of **currant bread** (if you can't find it, use any sliced **bread**)

a small handful of **baby spinach**

3½ oz **brie**, thinly sliced

salt and **freshly ground black pepper**

This is a great way to use leftover meat from Christmas Day. Or use roasted chicken—it works just as well. However, do make your own cranberry sauce. It is infinitely nicer than anything you can buy and really easy. In December, we serve a Christmas wrap—a three-meat triumph of ham hock, turkey, and pork-and-sage stuffing.

For the sauce, combine the sugar and orange juice in a saucepan and bring to a boil. Stir in the cranberries and clementine or satsuma zest. Simmer until the cranberries are tender but not falling apart: 5–6 minutes for frozen or 8–10 minutes for fresh. Remove from the heat and let cool. The sauce will thicken as it cools.

For the sandwich, melt the butter in a skillet over medium heat. Add the turkey meat and gently reheat for 5–6 minutes, until piping hot. Season to taste, then place in a bowl.

In the same pan, without wiping it clean, toast the bread slices for a couple of minutes on each side until light golden. Transfer to two plates.

Assemble the sandwiches. Divide the spinach between two slices of the toasted bread. Top each with half the sliced brie and turkey, then add a generous spoonful of the cranberry sauce. (Any leftover sauce can be stored in an airtight container in the refrigerator for up to 1 week or in the freezer for up to 2 months.) Top the sandwiches with the remaining slices of bread, then cut in half and eat immediately.

BANH MI

SERVES 4

PREP TIME: 20 MIN * COOK TIME: 10 MIN

DF | NF

a splash of **neutral cooking oil**

3 **pork chops**, fat trimmed off

FOR THE PICKLES:

2 large or 3 small **carrots**, peeled and julienned into thin matchsticks or ribbons

1 **daikon radish** (about 10½ oz), peeled and julienned into thin matchsticks or ribbons

½ cup **rice vinegar**

1 tablespoon **superfine sugar**

salt

FOR THE PORK SAUCE:

2 tablespoons **soy sauce**

1 clove of **garlic**, crushed

¼ teaspoon **superfine sugar**

½ teaspoon **Chinese five-spice**

TO ASSEMBLE:

4 small **French baguettes** (or use **Vietnamese baguettes** if you can find them)

good-quality **mayonnaise**

3½ oz **chicken** or **pork liver pâté**

Sriracha sauce

12 thick slices of **cucumber**

2 **scallions**, thinly sliced on an angle

fresh cilantro leaves

Banh mi started life as a legacy from the French colonization of Vietnam (not in itself a cause for celebration). The pâté is obviously a French ingredient and the bread is a softer Vietnamese version of the French baguette, made with rice flour, but you can use an ordinary baguette. If you don't want to use pork, try the Crispy Tofu on page 145, the panko-crumbed chicken on page 137, roasted duck, or grilled sliced eggplant, all of which work with the sauce below.

First, make the pickles. Put the carrots and daikon into a colander and sprinkle with a pinch of salt. Toss, let stand for a few minutes, then make the pickling liquid by stirring together the vinegar, sugar, 1 teaspoon of salt, and ½ cup of boiling water. Squeeze out the vegetables, place in a clean jar or bowl (see Tip), and pour over the pickling liquid. Let stand while you make the sandwiches, or store in the refrigerator until ready to use—the longer you leave them, the more intense the flavor.

Put a wide skillet over medium heat. Add a splash of oil, then when shimmering hot, add the chops and cook for about 4 minutes on each side, depending on their thickness, until golden brown and cooked through.

While the pork cooks, mix all the pork sauce ingredients together with a tablespoon of water. Remove the pork from the pan and cut into ½-inch strips, then return to the pan along with the sauce and cook for 1 minute. Transfer to a bowl while you make the sandwiches (if the pork strips overcook in the pan, the meat will be tough).

Slice the baguettes in half and spread one side of each with mayo and one side with the pâté. To the mayo side, add a good squirt of Sriracha sauce, 3 cucumber slices, a spoonful of the pickles, and some scallions and cilantro leaves. Add one quarter of the pork per baguette, and a little of its sauce, then dig in.

≡ TIP ≡

The pickled carrot and daikon radish will keep in the refrigerator for several weeks, sealed in a spotlessly clean and sterilized screw-top jar.

SARDINE BOCADILLOS

SERVES 2

PREP TIME: 2 MIN

DF | NF | SoF

1 **sourdough baguette**, halved

1 small clove of **garlic**, halved crosswise

1 ripe **tomato**, finely sliced or diced

2–4 **pickled hot** or **mild green chilies**, ideally **piquillo**, sliced

1 (3¾-oz) **can sardine fillets in olive oil** (choose the best quality you can find, Spanish if possible)

extra virgin olive oil, for drizzling

salt and **freshly ground black pepper**

Bocadillos are long, filled crusty rolls from Spain. They often contain nothing more than a whisper of thinly sliced jamon, or some slivers of chorizo, but others are more substantial and contain slices of leftover onion-and-potato omelet (tortilla) or fried calamari rings and aioli.

Split the baguette in half lengthwise. Rub each cut side with the cut side of the garlic clove. Pile the bread with the tomato pieces, then the pickled chilies.

Top with the sardine fillets. If the sardines are in excellent-quality oil, or happen to be salty, you may not need any more oil or any salt, but we love a little of both on top of the fillings, along with some black pepper.

Eat immediately.

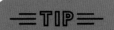

TIP

A famous version of this bocadillo adds a handful of potato chips on top of the fish. You could also add finely sliced scallion or slices of lightly pickled onion.

BLACK BEAN TACOS

SERVES 4

PREP TIME: 15 MIN ★ COOK TIME: 30 MIN

V | NF | SoF

a splash of **olive** or **vegetable oil**

1 **onion**, finely diced

2 cloves of **garlic**, crushed

2 teaspoons **tomato paste**

2 ripe **tomatoes**, finely chopped

½ **red chili**, hot or mild, finely chopped

2 (15-oz) cans **black beans in water** (do not drain)

a pinch of **dried oregano**

1 heaping teaspoon **unsweetened cocoa powder**

a pinch of **superfine sugar**

a pinch of **ground cinnamon**

1 heaping teaspoon **sweet** (not hot) **smoked paprika**

freshly squeezed lime juice, to taste

salt and **freshly ground black pepper**

TO SERVE:

8 small **corn** or **wheat tortillas**, warm

⅔ cup crumbled **feta cheese**

fresh cilantro leaves

optional sides/toppings: **Guacamole** (see page 195), **Slaw** of your choice (see pages 95–97), **Pink Pickled Onion**s (see page 185), **sour cream**

We love a legume at LEON, as you probably already know. Black beans have been on our menu, in the form of a Brazilian black bean stew, over brown rice, since 2016. Already cooked black beans are such a versatile ingredient that they often feature in our books.

Set a large saucepan over medium heat. When hot, add a splash of oil and the onion. Cook, stirring, for about 8 minutes, until translucent and just beginning to brown. Add the garlic and tomato paste along with a pinch of salt and cook, stirring, for 2–3 minutes, until neither the tomato paste nor garlic smells raw (the salt is to help prevent the garlic from burning).

Reduce the heat to low and add the diced tomatoes and chili. Cook, stirring often, for up to 5 minutes, until the tomatoes begin to break down. Add the beans and most of their liquid, along with the oregano, unsweetened cocoa powder, sugar, cinnamon, paprika, and some black pepper. Bring to a simmer and let bubble gently for 10 minutes, keeping an eye on the liquid levels and adding a little dash of water, if needed.

When ready, the beans should be saucy, but not soupy, so increase the heat to finish, if too wet. Remove from the heat. Taste and add more salt, if needed (remember the feta will add salt in a moment, too) and a squeeze of lime juice—just a little to start with, because it's just there to brighten up all the other flavors.

Serve piled onto warm tortillas, with the feta, cilantro leaves, and your favorite extras/toppings alongside.

HOW TO BUILD A TASTY TACO

Traditionally soft corn tortillas are used for tacos (although you can use hard shells if that's your thing). Look for ones made with a mix of corn and wheat, but whatever you find, don't buy massive wraps. Warm them as you serve. Leave a little space around the edge of the tortilla so the fillings won't fall off—as much—when you lift it to eat. Make sure you've got some crunch, especially if everything else is soft. We love slaws of all kinds (see recipes on pages 95–97), which also make meals better for your digestive biome, as well as oven-roasted, popped pumpkin seeds. Look for some tart, sharp ingredients to cut through richer ones, such as cooked meats, avo, or cheese: pickled chilies or Pink Pickled Onions (see page 185), freshly squeezed lime juice, fresh salsas such as Pico de Gallo (see page 195), or sour hot sauce will all work.

FILLING OPTIONS

Leftover roasted chicken, shredded, heated, and tossed in chipotle paste, with chopped scallions, chopped red chili, and freshly squeezed lime juice, topped with crumbled feta cheese or Mexican *queso fresco*.

Chunks of chorizo fried in the same pan as cubes of cooked potato, topped with pickled onions or finely chopped shallot and freshly squeezed lime juice.

Flash-fried skirt steak, sliced and dressed with Chimichurri Sauce (see page 106) and shredded cabbage.

Leftover roasted lamb, warmed in some broth, with crushed garlic, chopped red chili, ground cumin, and smoked paprika, finished with a squeeze of lime and Pink Pickled Onions (see page 185).

Quick fish tacos: Use store-bought fish sticks (or vegan fish-style sticks), cooked and sliced, then top the tacos with shredded green cabbage or slaw of your choice (see pages 95–97), sour cream or good-quality mayo of your choice (see pages 188–90), and Pico de Gallo (see page 195). Or switch the fish for freshly cooked shrimp.

Use the Crispy Tofu recipe on page 145 to top tacos along with Guacamole (see page 195), canned (drained) corn kernels, Pico de Gallo (see page 195), sliced radishes, and plenty of hot sauce.

Drain and rinse a 15-oz can of chickpeas (garbanzo beans), then toss in a little olive oil, ground cumin, salt, freshly ground black pepper, smoked paprika, and mild or hot chili powder before roasting at 400°F for 15 minutes. Then

pile onto tacos with shredded crisp lettuce, diced tomatoes, and Guacamole (see page 195).

In our *Fast Vegan* book, we have a recipe for crunchy fried avocado wedge tacos, with almond feta (see Tip, right), spicy cabbage slaw, and roasted pumpkin seeds.

Any leftover roasted vegetables can be reheated, then dressed in ground cumin, freshly squeezed lime juice, crushed garlic, and chopped fresh cilantro before being piled onto a tortilla, maybe with some roasted chickpeas (see above). You could even cover the tacos with grated or sliced cheese and then melt it under the broiler.

BREADS & ROLLS

=TIP=

To make almond feta, mix ¾ cup almond meal, 1 teaspoon freshly squeezed lemon juice, 2 tablespoons plain vegan yogurt, 1 tablespoon olive oil, 1 teaspoon fine salt, a pinch of garlic powder, and ¼ teaspoon vegan apple cider vinegar to form a crumbly paste. Squeeze out any excess liquid, if necessary, before serving.

SPICED LAMB FLATBREADS

SERVES 4

PREP TIME: 15 MIN * COOK TIME: 11–44 MIN

SoF

2 teaspoons **ground cumin**

1 teaspoon **ground coriander**

½ **onion**, finely chopped

1 tablespoon **tomato paste**

1 ripe **tomato**, seeded and chopped

1 **roasted red pepper from a jar**, drained and rinsed if in liquid, finely chopped

2 cloves of **garlic**, crushed

6 sprigs of **fresh flat-leaf parsley**, leaves picked and finely chopped

1 lb good-quality **ground lamb** (not low fat)

¾ teaspoon **salt**

cornmeal, for dusting

2 tablespoons **pine nuts** (optional)

freshly ground black pepper

Tzatziki (see page 194) and **lemon wedges**, to serve

FOR THE DOUGH:

2 cups **all-purpose flour**, plus extra for dusting

2 cups **'Italian "00" flour** (or if you can't find it, another 2 cups all-purpose flour)

2 teaspoons **active dry yeast**

1 teaspoon **superfine sugar**

1 teaspoon **salt**

1 cup **lukewarm water**

1½ tablespoons **olive oil**

These topped flatbreads are our version of lahmacun, a Turkish street food that Rebecca fell in love with when she was working in Istanbul. We've used the dough from our SuperFast Pizza (see page 67), so it only needs a short rise (but you must use active dry yeast). A little tomato, cucumber, and onion salad on the side would be just right.

As early as possible, heat the oven to its highest setting and place a pizza pit or a couple of up-turned baking pans in it to heat up.

Mix together the dough ingredients with a spoon in a large bowl. Then knead, using your hands, for about 5 minutes, into a smooth and elastic dough. Put back into the bowl and set aside somewhere warm for 10 minutes or until puffy.

For the topping, use a food processor to blend together the spices, onion, tomato paste, raw tomato, roasted pepper or pepper paste, and garlic until you have a coarse puree. Transfer to a bowl and add the parsley, lamb, salt, and some pepper. Use your hands to combine everything until you have a pastelike mixture.

Divide the rested dough into four balls and roll or stretch out one or two (depending on how many you can cook at a time) to 8-inch disks. Remove the pizza pit or baking pan(s) from the oven and dust with cornmeal to prevent sticking, then slide the disks on top. Working quickly, dot one quarter of the topping thinly across each crust. Sprinkle over one quarter of the pine nuts, if using.

Place the lahmacun in the oven and cook for 11 minutes, until the crust turns golden, the topping is bubbling, the meat is cooked through, and the bottom is pale gold. Remove from the oven. Repeat to make the remaining lahmacun in the same way.

Serve hot, each with Tzatziki and a lemon wedge for squeezing over the top.

SUPERFAST PIZZA

MAKES 2
PREP TIME: 20 MIN ★ COOK TIME: 20–28 MIN
NF | SoF

¾ cup **tomato puree** or **tomato sauce**

1 clove of **garlic**, crushed

2 teaspoons **olive oil**

a pinch of **salt**

a pinch of **dried oregano**

about 2 balls of **mozzarella**, drained and sliced or torn into small chunks

toppings of your choice: sliced **chorizo** or **pepperoni** and **pickled chili peppers**; **goat cheese** with **walnuts**; **artichokes** (from a jar) with **capers**

cornmeal, for dusting

extra virgin olive oil, to serve

FOR THE DOUGH:

2 cups **all-purpose flour**, plus extra for dusting

2 cups **Italian "00" flour** (or if you can't find it, another 2 cups all-purpose flour)

2 teaspoons **active dry yeast**

1 teaspoon **superfine sugar**

1 teaspoon **salt**

1 cup **lukewarm water**

1½ tablespoons **olive oil**

When we heard about pizza with a ten-minute rise, we were dubious, but this honestly works. The trick is using active dry (or instant) yeast.

As early as possible, heat the oven to its highest setting and place a pizza pit or a couple of up-turned baking pans in it to heat up.

Mix together the dough ingredients with a spoon in a large bowl. Then knead with your hands for 5 minutes into a smooth, elastic dough. Put back into the bowl and set aside somewhere warm for 10 minutes. It should feel slightly puffy when ready.

Make the sauce by mixing together the tomato puree or sauce, garlic, olive oil, salt, and oregano. Prepare any toppings.

When ready, divide the dough into two equal balls, then either stretch one out, using your knuckles under the dough to gently shape and thin the dough, or roll out into a 12-inch disk (rolling means less-to-no crust, so stretching is better but requires practice; ours are often less than perfect).

Remove the hot pit or one of the baking pans from the oven and dust it with cornmeal. Slide the dough crust onto the pit using your hands and a large spatula. Working fast, use the back of a spoon to smear 3–4 tablespoons of sauce thinly over the crust (too thick and the crust will be soggy). Dot the cheese sparingly over the sauce and add any remaining toppings over the top. Cook for 10–14 minutes.

Remove from the oven and check the crust is firm and pale gold. Transfer the pizza to a board before repeating with the remaining dough and toppings. The crust can be crunchy, so we like to brush it with a little extra virgin olive oil before serving.

CRISPY BLACK KALE & BABY BROCCOLI WRAP

SERVES 4

PREP TIME: 10 MIN * COOK TIME: 15–20 MIN

V | NF | SoF

FOR THE VEGETABLES:

9 oz **baby broccoli**

7 oz **black kale**

¼ cup **extra virgin olive oil**

1 teaspoon **dried red pepper flakes**

a couple of pinches of **salt**

5 cranks of **freshly ground black pepper**

FOR THE HARISSA YOGURT:

1 cup **Greek yogurt**

¼ cup **rose harissa paste**

salt and **freshly ground black pepper**

TO SERVE:

4 **flatbreads**

⅔ cup crumbled **feta cheese**

a big handful of **pomegranate seeds**

a big handful of **Pink Pickled Onions**
    (see page 185)

When Jack was testing recipes on his friends, this was the runaway winner. Harissa yogurt goes with (almost) anything that has been grilled or roasted, including this delicious roasted black kale and baby broccoli.

Heat the oven to 350°F.

For the vegetables, slice the baby broccoli lengthwise so that they are all a uniform size. Remove the black kale leaves from the thick stems, and put everything into a roasting pan. Drizzle the olive oil over the veg, sprinkle with the dried red pepper flakes, salt, and pepper, and mix well. Roast for 15–20 minutes, turning occasionally and making sure the ends of the vegetables don't brun.

While the veggies are in the oven, make the harissa yogurt. Combine the yogurt and harissa paste in a bowl and season to taste.

Toast each flatbread in a smoking hot, dry, nonstick skillet for about 30 seconds on each side, stacking them up on a plate to keep warm.

To assemble the wraps, spoon a generous dollop of harissa yogurt into the middle of each flatbread and smear evenly lengthwise. Pile up the roasted veg and top with crumbled feta and a sprinkling of pomegranate seeds and pink pickled onions. Roll up and eat.

GRILLED "CHEESE" SANDWICHES

ZUCCHINI, WALNUT & MINT

SERVES 2

PREP TIME: 5 MIN * COOK TIME: 15 MIN

DF | V | Ve | SoF

¼ cup **extra virgin olive oil**

3 cloves of **garlic**, thinly sliced

1 **zucchini**, halved lengthwise and cut into ¼-inch-thick semicircles

4 slices of **sourdough bread**

¼ cup **tahini**, well stirred

a large handful of **walnuts**, coarsely chopped

a large handful of **fresh mint leaves**, coarsely chopped

zest of 1 **unwaxed lemon**

agave syrup, to serve (optional)

salt and **freshly ground black pepper**

Jack's girlfriend is a committed cheese lover and never thought a vegan grilled "cheese" sandwich would work. But she took one bite of this and reluctantly admitted, "Yeah, this is actually tasty."

Place a large, nonstick skillet over medium-high heat and add a tablespoon of the oil. Add the garlic and fry for about 1 minute, until fragrant. Add the zucchini slices, season with a pinch of salt, then cook for 8–10 minutes, until softened. Transfer to a plate and set aside.

Wipe out the pan and put over medium heat with another tablespoon of oil. When hot, add the bread and cook for 1–2 minutes, until light brown underneath.

Transfer to two plates, cooked side up, and spread the tahini over two slices of toasted bread (one slice for each sandwich). Season each with a pinch of salt and a few twists of black pepper. Top each with half the fried zucchini, then sprinkle with the walnuts, chopped mint, and lemon zest, and add a drizzle of agave syrup, if using. Top each sandwich with the remaining slices of bread, cooked side down.

Heat one more tablespoon of the oil in the skillet over medium heat and add the sandwiches. Cook for 3–4 minutes, until the bottom of each sandwich is golden brown. Add the remaining tablespoon of oil, flip the sandwiches, and cook for 3–4 minutes, until the other side is golden brown.

Remove from the pan, cut each sandwich in half, and serve immediately.

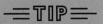
FONTINA, SAGE & PROSCIUTTO

SERVES 2

PREP TIME: 5 MIN * COOK TIME: 10 MIN

NF | SoF

3 tablespoons **butter**

4 slices of **sourdough bread**

8 slices of **prosciutto**

8 large **fresh sage leaves**

5 oz **fontina cheese**, thinly sliced

a few twists of **freshly ground black pepper**

Jack loves this grilled sandwich, especially the way the sage leaves turn crispy in the melting cheese (unreal).

Put a large, nonstick skillet over medium heat and add a tablespoon of the butter. Swirl it around the pan until it stops foaming. Add the bread and cook for about 2 minutes, until light brown on only one side. Transfer to a plate, cooked side up.

Layer two slices of the bread (one slice for each sandwich) each with 4 slices of prosciutto, 4 sage leaves, and half the cheese, then season with pepper. Top each sandwich with the remaining slices of bread, cooked side down.

Melt one more tablespoon of butter in the pan over medium heat and add the sandwiches. Cover with a lid to help the cheese melt quicker and cook for 3–4 minutes, until the bottom of each sandwich is golden brown. Remove the lid, add the remaining tablespoon of butter, flip the sandwiches, and cook for another 3–4 minutes, until the other side is golden brown and the cheese is melted.

Remove from the pan, cut each sandwich in half, and serve immediately.

FETA, HONEY & ALMOND

SERVES 2
PREP TIME: 5 MIN ★ COOK TIME: 10 MIN
V | SoF

3 tablespoons **butter**

4 slices of **sourdough bread**

¼ cup **tahini**, well stirred

2 tablespoons **honey**

leaves picked from 4 sprigs of **fresh thyme**

1 cup crumbled **feta cheese**

a handful of roasted **almonds**, coarsely
   chopped

Nutty tahini, tangy feta, and sweet honey combine to create this particularly tempting grilled cheese sandwich.

Put a large, nonstick skillet over medium heat and add a tablespoon of the butter. Swirl it around the pan until it stops foaming. Add the bread slices and cook for about 2 minutes, until light brown underneath.

Transfer to two plates, cooked side up, and spread the tahini over two slices of toasted bread (one slice for each sandwich). Drizzle the honey over them. Sprinkle the thyme leaves over the slices, then top with the feta and chopped almonds. Top each sandwich with the remaining slices of bread, cooked side down.

Melt one more tablespoon of butter in the pan over medium heat and add the sandwiches. Cover with a lid to help the cheese melt quicker and cook for 3–4 minutes, until the bottom of each sandwich is golden brown. Remove the lid, add the remaining tablespoon of butter, flip the sandwiches, and cook for another 3–4 minutes, until the other side is golden brown and the cheese is melted.

Remove from the pan, cut each sandwich in half, and serve immediately.

TIP

For an oozy, tangy, cheesy treat, we also love fig preserves, goat cheese, and thyme. Perfect for a lazy brunch.

COMTÉ, THYME & CARAMELIZED ONION

SERVES 2

PREP TIME: 5 MIN * COOK TIME: 1 HOUR

V | NF | SoF

4 tablespoons **butter**

3 **red onions**, thinly sliced

½ tablespoon **red wine vinegar**

1 teaspoon packed **light brown sugar**

4 slices of **sourdough bread**

leaves picked from 4 sprigs of **fresh thyme**

1½ cups shredded **Comté cheese** (if you can't find Comté cheese, you can use Gruyère cheese)

salt and **freshly ground black pepper**

This is inspired by Internet food legend J. Kenji López-Alt. It's decadent and rich and tastes like a French onion soup sandwich. Glorious.

Heat 1 tablespoon of the butter in a large skillet over medium-low heat. Add the onions, season, and cook, stirring frequently, for about 45 minutes, until a rich brown. Halfway through, add the vinegar and sugar. Taste for seasoning.

Transfer the onions to a bowl, wipe out the pan, and put back over medium heat with another tablespoon of butter. Swirl it around the pan until it stops foaming. Add the bread and cook on only one side for about 2 minutes, until light brown.

Transfer to two plates. Spread the onions over two slices of the toasted bread, sprinkle with thyme leaves, then top with the cheese. Top each sandwich with the remaining bread, cooked side down.

Melt one more tablespoon of butter in the pan over medium heat and add the sandwiches. Cover with a lid and cook for 3–4 minutes, until the bottom of each sandwich is golden brown. Remove the lid, add the remaining tablespoon of butter, flip the sandwiches, and cook for 3–4 minutes, until the other side is golden brown and the cheese is melted. Remove from the pan, cut each sandwich in half, and serve immediately.

LEON BACON & EGG MUFFIN

SERVES 2

PREP TIME: 5 MIN * COOK TIME: 15 MIN

NF | SoF

a dash of **vegetable oil**

4 slices of **unsmoked lean bacon** (nitrite-free if possible)

2 **English muffins**, sliced in half

2 pats of **butter**

2 **eggs**

ketchup, to taste

a handful of **baby spinach**

salt and **freshly ground black pepper**

This is possibly the best way to start any day. On the LEON menu since 2004.

Restaurants have egg rings to make perfect, muffin-size eggs, but if you don't have one, fashion two from two long strips of foil about 4 inches wide. Fold each over on themselves to make two flat strips about 1¼ inches wide, then form each into a neat ring.

Set a large skillet (with a lid) over medium heat. Add a dash of oil and cook the bacon until done to your preference. Remove, set aside, and keep warm. Toast the muffins and keep warm.

Wipe out the pan, put it back onto the heat, set the two rings inside it, and put a pat of butter into each one. When the butter bubbles fiercely (it needs to be really hot), break an egg into a mug, then gently pour it into a ring. Repeat with the other egg and ring. Pour 2 tablespoons of water into the pan around the rings and cover with the lid. Cook the eggs for 2½ minutes—the aim is to have a soft, but not runny, yolk so that it doesn't ooze out of the muffin.

While the eggs cook, squirt a little ketchup onto each muffin bottom half, then load a few spinach leaves and two slices of bacon on top.

Use a spatula to lift the cooked eggs out of the pan, trimming off any white that has leaked out of the foil rings, and place on top of the bacon. Season with salt and pepper, then top each with the other muffin half. Eat immediately.

HUEVOS RANCHEROS

SERVES 4

PREP TIME: 15 MIN * COOK TIME: 15 MIN

V | NF | SoF

neutral cooking oil

8 small **corn tortillas**, or 4 larger ones

8 **eggs**

1 (15-oz) can **refried beans** (or make your
own—see page 175)

about 1 tablespoon **chipotle paste**, or less
to taste (optional)

¼ cup crumbled **feta cheese**

fresh cilantro leaves, to garnish

FOR THE SALSA ROJA:

4 ripe **tomatoes**

1 **shallot** or ¼ **onion**, cut into chunks

¼–2 **hot green chilies** (ideally fresh
jalapeños), seeded or not, to taste

1 clove of **garlic**, cut into chunks

½ teaspoon **apple cider vinegar** (optional,
add if you want to store the salsa)

a pinch of **salt**

*We owe much of this recipe to food writer Patrick Calhoun and his excellent
"Mexican Please" website. (Of course, there are dozens of variations: some say
beans and cheese are unnecessary; others would balk at our lack of avo or lime.
Whatever works for you.)*

First, make the salsa. Put the tomatoes into a dry saucepan and let them dry-roast,
turning often, for about 5 minutes, until they are charred in a few places. Remove
with tongs, then cut them into quarters and put into a sieve to cool and drain,
pressing gently with the back of a spoon to remove some of the excess liquid.

When cool enough to handle, scoop out and discard the seeds and core. Put the
tomato pieces into a blender with all the other salsa ingredients (include the vinegar
only if you plan to store it—see Tip), starting with the ¼ chili and then adding
more, or all of them, to taste. The sauce should be spicy, tart, and a little chunky.
Try to avoid blending it so much that it becomes pale and frothy. Pour into a small
saucepan, set over medium heat, and simmer gently until ready to serve.

Put a large skillet over high heat. Add a splash of oil and, when it's really shimmering
hot, add 2–4 tortillas or as many as will fit in a single layer. Cook for 20–30 seconds,
until lightly browned, then flip and repeat. Drain on a plate lined with paper towels.
Repeat until all are cooked. Keep warm.

Reduce the heat. When the pan is no longer scorchingly hot, fry the eggs to your
preference, adding more oil as needed. Meanwhile, warm the refried beans in a
saucepan and stir in the chipotle paste. To serve, spread each tortilla with some of
the refried beans, then top with a fried egg. Spoon about a tablespoonful of the
salsa over each egg (don't use too much or it will make the tortillas soggy). Sprinkle
with the feta and cilantro. Eat immediately.

≡TIP≡

This makes more salsa than you will need, but it keeps well in an airtight container in the refrigerator for up to 3 days, or freeze it in small portions for up to 1 month, so you always have it available for a quick weekend brunch. Defrost (if frozen) and warm through gently before use.

NELL'S JAZZY BEANS

SERVES 4

PREP TIME: 10 MIN ★ COOK TIME: 5 MIN

DF | V | Ve | NF | SoF

¾ cup can **baked beans in tomato sauce**

1 teaspoon **chipotle paste**

1 slice of good-quality **bread** (such as **sourdough**), toasted

butter or **vegan alternative**, for spreading

2 teaspoons minced **shallot**, **scallion**, or **fresh chives**

¼–½ **avocado**, peeled, pitted, and diced (see page 87 for dicing technique)

a few **fresh cilantro leaves**

freshly squeezed lime juice, to taste

hot sauce, to taste

Baked beans on toast is the UK's ultimate fast food, but it can be a little dull. Rebecca (a freelance writer who is often working alone for long periods) makes this spiced-up version all the time. When she put a picture of this recipe on Instagram, her friend Nell commented, saying that in her house it's known as jazzy beans. And they are very jazzy. If you don't like baked beans, use canned plain navy beans and use some of the water from the can to make a sauce with the chipotle paste.

Warm the beans in a small saucepan. Stir through the chipotle paste, then taste and decide if you'd like more smoky heat. When you're happy, toast the bread and spread with butter or a vegan alternative. Pour the bean mixture onto the toast, then sprinkle with the chopped shallot, scallion, or chives, avocado, and cilantro leaves.

Squeeze a little lime juice over the top (but don't go crazy) and add a splash of hot sauce. Eat immediately.

SALADS

NOT NIÇOISE

SERVES 4

PREP TIME: 12 MIN * COOK TIME: 17 MIN

WF | GF | DF | V | NF | SoF

6 oz **new** or **baby potatoes**, quartered

2 cups **fava beans**, shelled, blanched, and skinned, or 2 cups long **green beans**, trimmed, or a mixture

4 **eggs**

1 **cucumber**, seeded and diced

16 **cherry tomatoes**, quartered

1 **green bell pepper**, seeded and diced

15 **black olives**, pitted and coarsely chopped

1 (15-oz) **can chickpeas (garbanzo beans)**, drained and rinsed

2 big handfuls of **mixed, soft salad greens**, coarsely chopped or torn, if large

4 sprigs of **fresh basil**, leaves picked and torn, if large

FOR THE DRESSING:

2 tablespoons **capers** in vinegar or brine, rinsed, drained, and finely chopped

3 sprigs of **fresh parsley**, leaves picked and minced

⅓ cup **extra virgin olive oil**

1 clove of **garlic**, crushed to a paste with the flat of a knife blade

2 teaspoons **sherry vinegar**

salt and **freshly ground black pepper**

In an attempt to cook more sustainably, Rebecca doesn't eat meat or fish on weekdays, so she is often to be found adapting recipes to make them vegetarian—this is one of her successful experiments.

Put the quartered potatoes into a saucepan of boiling, salted water and cook for about 12 minutes or until tender. About 2 minutes before the end of cooking, add the green beans, if using. Drain and set aside.

Bring another saucepan of water to a boil and gently add the eggs. Cook for 7½ minutes—for a slightly soft, creamy yolk and fairly firm whites. Drain and cool immediately in cold water. When cool enough to handle, peel and cut each egg into six wedges.

Put all the salad ingredients, except the eggs but including the warm potatoes and fava or green beans, into a large mixing bowl.

Mix all the dressing ingredients together in a small bowl and season with salt and pepper to taste. Add about half the dressing to the salad bowl and gently toss everything together.

Transfer the salad to a large serving platter and spread out. Arrange the egg wedges on top and drizzle over the remaining dressing to taste.

Eat immediately.

⎯ TIP ⎯

Chaat masala spice mix is now easy to find in large grocery stores—if you have some, sprinkle a tiny pinch over the salad just before serving. Swap the chickpeas for cooked lentils or beans, if you want, but don't roast them.

BAKED PANEER & WARM CHICKPEAS

SERVES 4

PREP TIME: 20 MIN ★ COOK TIME: 20 MIN

WF | GF | V | NF | SoF

½ teaspoon **ground turmeric**

1½ teaspoons **ground cumin**

1 teaspoon **ground coriander**

2 teaspoons **garlic powder**

½ teaspoon **dried red pepper flakes**,
    or to taste

½ teaspoon **sweet smoked paprika**

½ teaspoon **fine salt**

3 tablespoons **vegetable** or **coconut oil**

1 (15-oz) can of **chickpeas (garbanzo
    beans)**, drained and rinsed

8 oz **paneer**, cut into ½-inch cubes

2 tablespoons **pumpkin seeds**

1⅓ cups shredded **kale** or **pointed cabbage**
    (¼-inch-thick strips)

FOR THE SALAD:

6 **radishes**, very finely sliced

20 sprigs of **watercress** (about 2 oz),
    washed and woody stems removed

1 **scallion**, finely chopped

freshly squeezed lime juice, to taste

1 small **raw beet**, peeled and very, very
    finely sliced (use a mandoline, if you can)

FOR THE YOGURT DRESSING:

¼ cup **Greek yogurt**

freshly squeezed lime juice, to taste

a pinch of **ground cumin**

salt and **freshly ground black pepper**

A big salad, full of big flavors. Usually paneer is pan-fried, but baking it like this stops the spices from burning. This partners wonderfully with the Bhaji Burgers on page 20.

Heat the oven to 400°F.

Mix all the spices and salt together in a large bowl and season with pepper. Grease two nonstick baking pans with a little of the oil, then add the rest of the oil to the spices to form a paste. Add the chickpeas and paneer cubes and toss gently, making sure not to break the paneer, until everything is well coated.

Transfer this mixture to the two baking pans and spread out in a single layer. Bake for 10 minutes.

Remove the pans from the oven and add the pumpkin seeds and shredded kale or cabbage. Toss gently, turning each piece of paneer—use a spatula if any have stuck. Return to the oven for another 10 minutes. Remove and set aside to cool a little.

Prepare all the salad ingredients, then the dressing—whisking together the yogurt, ground cumin, and a teaspoon or so of lime juice with a pinch of salt and some black pepper. Add a tablespoon or so of water to thin it enough so that you can pour it. Taste and add more lime juice or salt, as needed.

To serve, toss together the radishes, watercress, and scallion with a little lime juice in a bowl. Separately, squeeze a little lime juice over the beet (or toss it all in all at once, but the beet will dye the salad pink). Spread out the salad vegetables on a big, wide platter. Sprinkle the warm paneer and chickpeas over the top, then either drizzle the dressing over the top or serve it on the side. Eat immediately and don't leave any leftovers! (Cooked paneer doesn't benefit from time in the refrigerator.)

PEA & QUINOA KISIR

SERVES 5–6 AS A SIDE

PREP TIME: 15 MIN, PLUS COOLING * COOK TIME: 15 MIN

WF | GF | DF | V | Ve | SoF

¾ cup uncooked **quinoa**

1 cup **frozen peas** (you can use fresh, in season, but they will need another 5 minutes cooking)

⅓ **cucumber**, finely chopped

1 **scallion** or a handful of **fresh chives**, minced

⅓ cup chopped **walnuts**

3 tablespoons **pomegranate seeds**

a bushy sprig of **fresh mint**, leaves picked and finely chopped

3–4 stems of **fresh parsley**, leaves picked and finely chopped

½ teaspoon **pomegranate molasses**

2 tablespoons **extra virgin olive oil**

salt and **freshly ground black pepper**

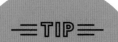

=TIP=

If quinoa isn't your thing, this works with bulgur wheat (which is what kisir usually contains) or couscous.

The LEON Original Salad has been pea and quinoa since before people knew how to say quinoa. Rebecca makes this and keeps it in the refrigerator, grazing on it over a couple days. Which is the definition of fast food, no?

Great as a side with sandwiches (grilled or otherwise) or on its own topped with more nuts, feta cheese, or any of our hummuses (hummi?) on pages 186–87.

Rinse the quinoa in a fine sieve under running water. Bring 2½ cups of water to a boil in a large saucepan and add the quinoa. Simmer for about 15 minutes or until the quinoa is tender, adding the peas for the last 2 minutes of cooking.

Drain in the fine sieve again, then set the quinoa and peas aside to cool.

When cool, put into a serving bowl. Add the cucumber, scallion or chives, walnuts, pomegranate seeds, mint, and parsley. Separately, mix together the pomegranate molasses and olive oil with a pinch of salt and a little pepper (it won't mix well; don't worry too much).

Pour the dressing over the salad and toss thoroughly. Taste, adding more salt if needed, then serve.

AVOCADO & BUTTER LETTUCE

SERVES 4 AS A SIDE
PREP TIME: 10 MIN
WF | GF | DF | V | Ve | NF | SoF

1 head of **butter** or **butterhead lettuce**, leaves separated, core trimmed away, washed, leaves left whole or chopped

1 **avocado**

2 teaspoons finely chopped **fresh chives**

FOR THE DRESSING:

2 tablespoons **extra virgin olive oil**

2 teaspoons **freshly squeezed lemon juice**

a pinch of **salt**

This is a traditional side to brasserie-style hamburgers. Try it with the Super Simple Hamburger on page 11 or the LOVe At-Home Vegan Burger on page 12. You can find butter or butterhead lettuce in the grocery stores and farmer's markets, but any lettuce with soft and floppy, rather than crisp, leaves works.

Put the lettuce into a large serving bowl. Cut the avocado in half and remove the pit. Then—with the flesh still in the skin—cut the flesh into cubes, letting the knife press against the skin but without cutting through. Run a spoon between the flesh and the skin, letting the cubes of avocado fall into the bowl. Add the chives.

Whisk together the oil, lemon juice, and salt for the dressing in a small bowl. Taste and add more lemon juice or salt, if you think it needs it. Pour half the dressing over the salad and gently toss. Add the rest, as needed.

Serve immediately, otherwise the avocado will turn brown.

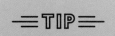

TIP

Try this with flakes of shaved Parmesan cheese or crumbled feta cheese on top.

═TIP═

If you want to make your own crispy onions, finely slice 2 onions. Add 3 tablespoons of vegetable or olive oil to a skillet over low-medium heat, add the onions, and cook for 20–25 minutes, stirring often and adding more oil if needed, until deep brown and crisp (but not charred). Remove to a plate lined with paper towels and let cool before using.

KOSHARI

¾ cup **long-grain white rice**, rinsed in cold running water

1 tablespoon **olive oil**

1 teaspoon **ground cumin**

5 oz **dried ditalini** or **macaroni**

2 cups drained and rinsed, canned or cooked **green** or **brown lentils**

1 (15-oz) can of **chickpeas (garbanzo beans)**, drained and rinsed

about 2 cups **crispy fried onions** (from a package)

salt

FOR THE SAUCE:

a splash of **olive oil**

1 **onion**, finely diced

3 cloves of **garlic**, crushed

1½ cups **tomato puree** or **tomato sauce**

1 teaspoon **dried red pepper flakes**, or to taste, plus an extra pinch to serve

2 teaspoons **baharat spice mix**, or 1 teaspoon each of **paprika** and **ground cumin**, plus an extra pinch of each to serve

2 teaspoons **sherry vinegar** or **apple cider vinegar** (Ve if needed)

salt and **freshly ground black pepper**

Koshari is a street food dish from Egypt made with lentils, chickpeas, a tangy, spiced tomato sauce, and crunchy onions. Rebecca first learned about it from one of her heroes, food writer Anissa Helou. It's excellent with the Spiced Lamb Burger on page 16.

In a large saucepan for which you have a lid, add the oil and set over medium heat. Add the cumin and toast briefly, then add the rice and and 1½ cups of water. Add a pinch of salt and the lid. Bring to a simmer and cook for 9 minutes. Add the pasta and scant ½ cup of boiling water and cook for 5 minutes. Remove the pan from the heat, add the lentils and chickpeas, stir through, then cover with a lid and let the pan stand for 5 minutes. The legumes will heat through and the pasta will finish cooking in this time.

While the rice is cooking, make the sauce. Pour a splash of oil into a saucepan set over low-medium heat. Add the onion and a pinch of salt and cook for about 6 minutes, until beginning to soften. Add the garlic and cook for 2 minutes, then add the rest of the sauce ingredients, including some black pepper to taste, and simmer gently for 5 minutes.

To serve, stir half the crispy onions into the rice-and-legume mixture (which shouldn't need draining), and reserve the rest as a garnish. Divide the rice between two shallow bowls, then top with the sauce and the remaining crispy onions. Dig in.

ARUGULA, PINE NUT & PARMESAN

SERVES 4 AS A SIDE
PREP TIME: 10 MIN
WF | GF | V | SoF

A sophisticated salad—wonderful at making burgers or nuggets fancier, or if you want to impress someone.

FOR THE DRESSING:
2 tablespoons **extra virgin olive oil**
2 tablespoons good-quality **balsamic vinegar**
1 teaspoon **honey**
1 small clove of **garlic**, grated
a pinch of **salt**

FOR THE SALAD:
7 cups **baby arugula leaves**
¼ cup **pine nuts**, toasted
3½ oz **Parmesan cheese** (or use **vegetarian Parmesan-style cheese**), shaved
finely grated zest of ½ **unwaxed lemon**

In a small bowl, whisk together all the dressing ingredients. Taste for seasoning, adjust if necessary, and whisk again. Set aside.

In a large salad bowl, combine the arugula leaves and pine nuts. Stir through the dressing and top with the shaved Parmesan and lemon zest. Serve immediately.

LITTLE GEM & BLUE CHEESE

SERVES 4 AS A SIDE
PREP TIME: 10 MIN
WF | GF | V | SoF | NF

FOR THE DRESSING:
3 tablespoons **extra virgin olive oil**
1 tablespoon **lemon juice**
2 tablespoons finely chopped **chives**
a pinch of **salt**
freshly ground black pepper

FOR THE SALAD:
3 small heads of **Little Gem** or other **small butter lettuce**, quartered
1 cup crumbled **blue cheese**

Whisk together the dressing ingredients.

Put the lettuce into a serving bowl or on a platter and drizzle half the dressing over the greens, then gently toss. Sprinkle with the cheese, then drizzle over a little more of the dressing. Serve the salad immediately.

SALADS

BURRATA
WITH BALSAMIC STRAWBERRIES, BASIL & MINT

SERVES 4

PREP TIME: 15 MIN, PLUS MARINATING, IF YOU HAVE TIME

WF | GF | V | NF | SoF

2 cups hulled and quartered **fresh strawberries**

2 tablespoons good-quality **balsamic vinegar**

1 tablespoon **white sugar**

3 (3½-oz) balls of **burrata**

2 tablespoons **extra virgin olive oil**

a small handful each of **fresh basil** and **mint leaves**

a couple of pinches of **flaky sea salt,** or more to taste

a few twists of **freshly ground black pepper**

This is a great way to eat strawberries as a summer appetizer or salad. The tartness of the strawberries and vinegar is balanced by the rich creaminess of the burrata. If you can't find burrata, buffalo mozzarella works almost as well.

Mix the strawberries in a bowl with the vinegar and sugar. Cover and let marinate in the refrigerator for a few hours, if you have time.

When ready to serve, put the strawberries onto a serving platter. Split open the burrata balls and dollop the creamy cheese over the strawberries. Drizzle with the olive oil, tear over the basil and mint leaves, and sprinkle with the salt and pepper.

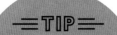

TIP

The strawberries, vinegar, and herbs also work especially well as a topping for vanilla ice cream or frozen yogurt as a dessert.

CLASSIC COLESLAW

SERVES 4 AS A SIDE

PREP TIME: 10 MIN, PLUS DRAINING, IF YOU HAVE TIME

WF | GF | DF | V | NF | SoF

2 cups cored and shredded **red** or **green cabbage**, or a mixture

1 **carrot**, peeled and cut into thin strips or shredded

2 **scallions**, finely chopped

2–3 tablespoons good-quality **mayonnaise**

1 teaspoon **Dijon mustard** (optional)

salt and **freshly ground black pepper**

Slaws not only taste delicious in wraps and alongside burgers, nuggets, and our "jack wings," adding crunch as well as flavor, they also introduce a welcome hit of raw veggies, which can help maintain a healthy digestive biome.

We are also known for our twist on coleslaw, which has kale in it: kaleslaw.

If you have time, put the cabbage and carrot into a colander and sprinkle with a pinch of salt. Toss, let drain for 5–10 minutes, then discard the liquid. If you don't have time, don't worry.

Put the vegetables into a large bowl. In a small bowl, mix 2 tablespoons of the mayo with the mustard, if using, and then use this to dress the coleslaw. If it looks even just a little dry—it should be rich and creamy, but not wet—add the remaining mayo and mix again. Season to taste with salt and pepper.

Eat immediately.

GRAZKA'S FENNEL SLAW

SERVES 4 AS A SIDE
PREP TIME: 10 MIN
WF | GF | DF | V | Ve | NF | SoF

1 **fennel** bulb

2 **celery stalks**

about ¼ **tart green apple** (such a **Granny Smith**), cored

1 tablespoon **freshly squeezed lemon juice**

2 tablespoons **extra virgin olive oil**

¼ teaspoon **Dijon mustard** (optional)

3 tablespoons finely chopped **fresh flat-leaf parsley**

2 teaspoons finely chopped **fresh chives**

a generous pinch of **salt**

freshly ground black pepper

Rebecca's friend Grazka is the kind of person who invites you for a casual barbecue, then whips out four kinds of meat, a vegan option, and seven salads. This is her version of an Ottolenghi salad, and it's even better than her beef ribs (which are awesome).

Ideally, slice the fennel, celery, and apple using a mandoline, but if not, slice them as thinly as possible, then mix together in a serving bowl.

Mix together the lemon juice, olive oil, and mustard, if using (the mustard is delicious, but equally, without it the vegetables all come through in their own right), then pour about half over the slaw. Toss well (the dressing stops it all from turning brown).

Add the herbs to the bowl along with the salt and some pepper. Toss again, then taste and decide if you'd like the rest of the dressing or more salt.

Eat immediately.

RED SLAW

SERVES 4 AS A SIDE

PREP TIME: 10 MIN

WF | GF | DF | V | Ve | NF | SoF

7 oz **green cabbage** (about 2 cups prepared)

1 **carrot, peeled**

3 tablespoons **ketchup**

2 teaspoons **apple cider vinegar** (Ve if needed)

1½ tablespoons **hot sauce** (or less, to taste)

plenty of **freshly ground black pepper**

This is our version of a Lexington or North Carolina red slaw—it's hot, tangy, crunchy, and delicious in burgers, as well as with pork dishes, or as a side.

Trim the cabbage and carrot, then shred the cabbage finely and chop the carrot finely, too (a trick is to cut the carrots into skinny strips with a julienne peeler, then chop the strips).

Mix together the ketchup, vinegar, hot sauce, and black pepper in a bowl, then toss the slaw with the sauce. Taste—it should be hot, sweet, and tangy, and it shouldn't need any salt.

Eat immediately.

PEAR, WALNUT & BLUE CHEESE

SERVES 4–6

PREP TIME: 15 MIN * COOK TIME: 5 MIN

WF | GF | V | SoF

FOR THE DRESSING:

3 tablespoons **extra virgin olive oil**

2 tablespoons good-quality **balsamic vinegar**

2 tablespoons **Dijon mustard**

1 tablespoon **honey**

juice of ½ **orange**

a pinch of **salt**

FOR THE SALAD:

1 cup **walnuts**

⅓ cup **dried cranberries**

2 ripe **pears**

7 cups **mixed salad greens**

1 cup crumbled **blue cheese** (**Stilton** or **Roquefort** both work well)

Perfect as an appetizer or a side. The tartness of the blue cheese is balanced nicely by the sweetness of the pear and cranberries. Pecans or toasted hazelnuts also work really well in this tasty salad.

In a small bowl, whisk together all the dressing ingredients. Taste for seasoning, adjust if necessary, and whisk again. Set aside.

To make the salad, toast the walnuts in a dry skillet over medium heat, turning often, for 4–5 minutes, until fragrant. Set aside to cool.

Coarsely chop the walnuts and dried cranberries. Core and slice the pears.

In a large bowl, combine the salad greens, walnuts, cranberries, pears, and crumbled blue cheese. Arrange on a platter and drizzle with the dressing. Serve immediately.

SEA BEANS & FENNEL

SERVES 4 AS A SIDE
PREP TIME: 5 MIN * COOK TIME: 5 MIN
WF | GF | DF | V | NF | SoF

3 tablespoons **extra virgin olive oil**

1 tablespoon **freshly squeezed lemon juice**

½ teaspoon **unwaxed lemon zest**

1 teaspoon **Dijon mustard**

1 teaspoon **honey**

a pinch of **salt**

⅔ cup **sea beans**

1 **fennel** bulb, thinly sliced (save the feathery leaves for garnish)

freshly ground black pepper

This is a light and refreshing salad, great served with grilled, barbecued, or baked fish. Alternatively, wrap it up in a flatbread with grilled salmon, monkfish, or—and why the heck not?—fish sticks, or any of our fried chicken alternatives on pages 160–65.

Whisk together the oil, lemon juice, lemon zest, mustard, honey, and salt in a small mixing bowl.

Bring a small saucepan of water to a boil and blanch the sea beans for 1 minute. Drain and refresh in a bowl of iced water. Drain and pat dry with paper towels.

Discard the tough outer leaves and core of the fennel and slice the rest as thinly as possible (ideally using a mandoline).

Put the sea beans and fennel into a bowl and stir through the dressing. Garnish with the feathery fennel leaves, sprinkle with black pepper, and serve.

=TIP=

Don't make this too far in advance, otherwise the fennel will turn brown.

TOMATO KACHUMBER

SERVES 4–6 AS A SIDE
PREP TIME: 10 MIN
WF | GF | DF | V | Ve | NF | SoF

8 fresh **plum tomatoes**

2 **red onions**

a handful of **fresh parsley**

2 teaspoons **ground cumin**

2 tablespoons **white wine vinegar**

2 tablespoons **extra virgin olive oil**, plus extra if necessary

about 1 teaspoon **salt**

5 cranks of **freshly ground black pepper**

Tart and tangy, this Indian salad goes well with any grilled meat or fish. Serve it alongside the Bhaji Burgers on page 20, the Spiced Lamb Burgers on page 16, or the Falafel & Harissa Wraps on page 26. Usually, it contains cucumber, so feel free to add some if you prefer.

Halve and seed the tomatoes, getting rid of the watery cores. Slice lengthwise into thin strips and put into a large bowl.

Peel and thinly slice the onions (use a mandoline if you have one). Add to the tomatoes along with the parsley leaves.

Add the cumin, vinegar, oil, salt, and pepper and stir to combine. If the salad looks a little dry, add a splash more oil.

Taste for seasoning, adjust, and mix again. Serve immediately.

ON THE STOVE

SKIRT STEAK WITH CHIMICHURRI

SERVES 4–6

PREP TIME: 5 MIN, PLUS RESTING ✳ COOK TIME: 10 MIN

WF | GF | DF | NF | SoF

2¼ lb **skirt steak**, trimmed of any excess fat and connective tissue, at room temperature
¼ cup **olive oil**
salt and **freshly ground black pepper**
Chimichurri, to serve (see page 191)

Skirt or hanger steak is sometimes known as the butcher's cut, because they used to keep it behind the counter for themselves. It's cheap but incredibly flavorful. It needs to be cooked quickly and over high heat, preferably a ripping hot barbecue. If not, a smoking hot cast iron grill pan will do, but don't forget to turn on your extractor fan. If you can't find skirt steak, look for a steak with some texture, such as sirloin.

Make sure the steak has come up to room temperature—remove it from the refrigerator at least 30 minutes before cooking.

Heat the barbecue grill, broiler pan, or cast iron grill pan until smoking hot.

Rub the steak with the olive oil and season generously with salt and pepper. Halve the steak if it's too big for your pan.

Put onto the rack or into the pan and cook for 4–5 minutes on each side for medium-rare. Resist the temptation to touch it and turn it only once, so that a beautiful, crunchy char develops on each side.

Remove and transfer to a cutting board, cover with aluminum foil, and let rest for 10 minutes.

Slice thinly, against the grain, and spoon some chimichurri over the steak to serve.

MACKEREL WITH CAPER BROWN BUTTER

SERVES 4

PREP TIME: 10 MIN * COOK TIME: 12 MIN

WF | GF | NF | SoF

1 stick (½ cup) **butter**, cut into small pieces

3 tablespoons **capers** in vinegar, rinsed, drained, and coarsely chopped

1 tablespoon finely chopped **fresh parsley**

a splash of **neutral cooking oil**

4–8 skin-on **mackerel fillets**, depending on their size and your hunger

salt and **freshly ground black pepper**

lemon wedges, to serve

Brown butter is made by almost burning butter in a small saucepan—the end result is a nutty, caramelized butter sauce. Adding capers turns it into an elegant sauce for any richly flavored fish, especially mackerel.

Although we usually love multitasking in the kitchen, with brown butter it's best to focus on just the pan it is in, because it can go from perfect to ruined in a matter of seconds—and anyway, it takes only 5 minutes to make. Put a small saucepan over low-medium heat. Add the butter and let melt. Next, let the butter foam up, stirring more or less constantly, so the solids don't catch and burn. Watch closely when the bubbling has subsided and a thick creamy foam has settled on the top, because it is almost ready—use a spoon to push back the foam to check the color of the butter. When golden, remove from the heat and pour into a bowl immediately, otherwise it will burn.

Add the capers and parsley and set the sauce aside while you cook the fish.

Place a large skillet over medium heat. Add a splash of oil and tilt the pan to spread it evenly across the bottom. Pat dry and then season the mackerel fillets all over with salt and pepper, then put them, skin side down, into the pan. Cook for about 3 minutes on each side, depending on thickness, until just cooked through (the fish will be just about flaking) and the skin is slightly browned and puckered.

Serve the mackerel on warm plates with a little of the caper sauce spooned over the fish and wedges of lemon on the side.

≡TIP≡

If you prefer whole (gutted and cleaned) mackerel, as we used here, season it all over and either broil under a hot broiler for 5 minutes on each side or bake in the oven at 375°F for 20–25 minutes.

SALMON WITH HERBED TAHINI

SERVES 4

PREP TIME: 10 MIN * COOK TIME: 10 MIN

WF | GF | DF | NF | SoF

vegetable oil, for cooking

4 skin-on **salmon fillets**

salt and **freshly ground black pepper**

lemon wedges, to serve

FOR THE TAHINI SAUCE:

⅓ cup **tahini**, well stirred

2 teaspoons finely chopped **fresh chives**

a sprig of **fresh dill**, leaves picked and
　finely chopped

a sprig of **fresh parsley**, leaves picked and
　finely chopped

a bushy sprig of **fresh basil**, leaves picked
　and finely chopped

8 **fresh mint leaves**, finely chopped

1 tablespoon **freshly squeezed lemon
　juice**, or to taste

1 small clove of **garlic**, crushed to a paste
　(blanch for 3 minutes in boiling water for
　a milder flavor)

a generous pinch of **salt**

This herb-and-sesame sauce is also good with roasted chicken, steamed broccoli, or grilled asparagus, or spooned over broiled halloumi. You can use it as a dressing over a hearty Middle Eastern or Mediterranean salad, too, either as it is or with a couple of tablespoons of yogurt stirred through. Or try adding feathery fennel leaves, dill, and/or tarragon to this summery green sauce. You do need to like the slightly bitter nuttiness of tahini to like this sauce (and Rebecca's husband certainly doesn't).

To make the tahini sauce, mix everything together in a small bowl or the jar of an immersion blender, checking no stems find their way in (otherwise, the sauce will be hard to blend and can be bitter or woody in flavor). Process, gradually adding 2–3 tablespoons of water until you get a smooth texture and it is about as thick as heavy cream. Taste and add more lemon or salt, as needed—it should be pretty tangy to cut through the rich salmon.

Pan-fry the salmon. Pour a little oil into the bottom of a skillet set over medium heat. Season the fish all over with salt and pepper. Cook the salmon, first skin side down, and then, when the skin is a deep golden color, turn and cook the other side. Depending on the thickness of the salmon, it will take 3–5 minutes on each side. Cook the uncooked fillet sides briefly, too, if you like your salmon thoroughly cooked through.

Serve immediately with lemon wedges and the tahini sauce on the side or drizzled over the fish.

LINGUINE WITH CLAMS

SERVES 4

PREP TIME: 10 MIN ★ COOK TIME: 12 MIN

DF | NF | SoF

14 oz **dried linguine**

¼ cup good-quality **extra virgin olive oil**, plus a little extra for drizzling

4 large cloves of **garlic**, thinly sliced

½ teaspoon **dried red pepper flakes**

2¼ lb **fresh clams in the shell**, rinsed (discard any with broken shells and tap any with open shells on the work surface—if they don't close immediately, throw them out)

⅔ cup **dry white wine**

juice of ½ **lemon**

a large bunch of **fresh parsley**, finely chopped

salt and **freshly ground black pepper**

crusty bread, to serve

≡TIP≡

This is the *bianco* version of the dish. For the *rosso* version, add ½ cup chopped cherry tomatoes along with the sliced garlic and red pepper flakes.

A classic seafood pasta from Campania, it is easy to make and bursting with flavor. It's made in a similar way to Spaghetti Aglio e Olio (see page 123) but with the addition of clams and white wine. Some people use spaghetti, but we prefer linguine, because it has more surface area to soak up the sauce.

Pasta isn't usually thought of as a fast food, but we disagree—what will you more likely cook when you need something quick and nourishing? (And remember, pasta was served as street food in places such as Naples back in the 1800s.)

Bring a large pot of heavily salted water to a boil. The water should be as salty as the sea. Add the linguine and cook for 1 minute less than the package directions.

While the linguine cooks, put the olive oil, garlic, and red pepper flakes into a cold skillet (one with a fitted lid) and bring up to heat over medium-high heat. Slowly cook the garlic for about 4 minutes, until softened, fragrant, and just starting to turn golden on the edges. Add the clams and white wine and immediately put on the lid. Give the pan a good shake and cook for 3–4 minutes, shaking every minute, until all or most of the clams have opened. Discard any that don't open.

When the pasta is ready, drain it, reserving a cupful of the cooking water, and transfer the pasta to the skillet. Add the lemon juice. Cook for another 1–2 minutes, tossing and stirring vigorously until a sauce starts to form and coat the linguine. If it is too dry, add a splash of the reserved pasta water. If it is too wet, increase the heat briefly and cook it off. You should be left with a glossy sauce.

Season to taste and stir through the parsley. Transfer to four bowls, drizzle with a little extra olive oil, and serve with crusty bread to mop up the juices. Trust us on that last part. You don't want to waste them.

WILD MUSHROOM PAPPARDELLE
WITH THYME & CRISPY SAGE

SERVES 4

PREP TIME: 5 MIN * COOK TIME: 15 MIN

V | NF | SoF

2 tablespoons **extra virgin olive oil**

14 oz **mixed fresh wild mushrooms,**
coarsely torn into large chunks

a few sprigs of **fresh thyme**, leaves picked

4 cloves of **garlic**, minced

2 tablespoons **butter**

2 teaspoons **freshly squeezed lemon juice**

14 oz **dried pappardelle pasta**

12 large **fresh sage leaves**

1 cup freshly grated **Parmesan cheese** (or
use **vegetarian Parmesan-style cheese**)

a large handful of **fresh parsley leaves,**
finely chopped

salt and **freshly ground black pepper**

The mushrooms add a deep, rich flavor, and crispy sage just makes everything better. Well, maybe not everything. But a lot of things.

Bring a large pot of heavily salted water to a boil. The water should be as salty as the sea.

Heat 1 tablespoon of the oil in a skillet over medium heat. Add the mushrooms and season with a teaspoon of salt. When the mushrooms start to release their water, after 4–5 minutes, add the thyme and garlic. Keep tossing for another 5–6 minutes as the mushrooms, garlic, and thyme start to caramelize. Add 1 tablespoon of the butter and cook for another 3–4 minutes, until everything is a nutty brown. Remove from the heat, check the seasoning, then add the lemon juice.

Meanwhile, cook the pappardelle in the pot of boiling salted water for 1 minute less than the package directions. While the pasta is cooking, heat the remaining butter in a small skillet until it stops foaming. Add the sage leaves, then cook for 1–2 minutes, until crispy and fragrant. Remove and set aside.

Drain the pasta, reserving a cupful of the cooking water. Add the pappardelle to the mushroom pan and put over medium heat. Add a splash of the reserved pasta water and half the Parmesan. Toss and stir constantly for 1–2 minutes or until a sauce begins to form and cling to the pasta. It should be creamy but without the need for cream. Add a little more pasta water, if necessary. Stir through the parsley.

Serve in four bowls, drizzled with the remaining oil and sprinkled with the remaining Parmesan and a few twists of black pepper. Finish with the crisp sage leaves.

RIGATONI WITH EASY TOMATO SAUCE

SERVES 4

PREP TIME: 5 MIN * COOK TIME: 20–25 MIN

V | NF | SoF

2 tablespoons **extra virgin olive oil**, plus extra for drizzling

1 **red onion**, thinly sliced

4 cloves of **garlic**, minced

a bunch of **fresh basil**, stems finely chopped, leaves coarsely chopped

2 (14½-oz) cans good-quality **diced tomatoes** (don't skimp, it's not worth it)

1 tablespoon red wine vinegar

1 lb **dried rigatoni**

2 oz **Parmesan cheese** (or **vegetarian Parmesan-style cheese**; ⅔ cup freshly grated)

salt and **freshly ground black pepper**

There's a reason this remains one of the most popular pasta dishes in the world. It's incredibly easy, tasty, and quick. A classic. You can use any pasta you want—penne or spaghetti are popular—but we like rigatoni, because it is a little chunkier and traps the sauce nicely.

Put a saucepan over medium heat and add the olive oil, onion, and a pinch of salt. Cook for 5–7 minutes, until softened and just starting to turn lightly golden. Stir in the garlic and basil stems and cook for another 2–3 minutes, until fragrant.

Pour in the tomatoes, add the vinegar, and continue cooking for 12–15 minutes. Taste for seasoning and add some salt and pepper. Stir in the basil leaves, then reduce the heat to low.

Meanwhile, bring a large pot of heavily salted water to a boil. The water should be as salty as the sea. Add the rigatoni and cook for 1 minute less than the package directions.

Drain the pasta, reserving a cupful of the cooking water, and add the pasta to the tomato sauce. Cook for another 1–2 minutes, stirring constantly, until the sauce is glossy and coating the pasta evenly. If it becomes a thick or sticky, add a splash of the reserved pasta water. Taste for seasoning one last time and adjust, if needed.

Transfer to four bowls, drizzle with a little extra olive oil, and grate the Parmesan over the top. Eat immediately.

ORECCHIETTE WITH BROCCOLI & CHILI SAUCE

SERVES 2

PREP TIME: 5 MIN ✳ COOK TIME: 20 MIN

NF | SoF

7 oz **dried orecchiette pasta**

¼ cup **extra virgin olive oil**, plus extra for drizzling

2 **canned anchovy fillets**, drained

4 cloves of **garlic**, thinly sliced

1 **red chili**, seeded and thinly sliced, or a generous pinch of **dried red pepper flakes**

1 large head of **broccoli**, broken into small florets of equal size

⅔ cup freshly grated **Parmesan cheese**, plus a little extra for garnish

a large handful of **fresh parsley leaves**, finely chopped

salt and **freshly ground black pepper**

This is one of Jack's favorite pastas and an excellent way to get more plants into your diet. The trick is to steam the broccoli in seasoned olive oil and pasta water until mushy. It emulsifies into a wonderful sauce—sounds weird, but it really works. Make sure you use a skillet that has a lid. Orecchiette means "little ears" in Italian, and is the perfect pasta for this dish, because little puddles of sauce pool in the middle of each one.

Bring a large pot of heavily salted water to a boil. It should be as salty as the sea. Add the orecchiette and cook for 1 minute less than the package directions.

Meanwhile, place 3 tablespoons of the oil, the anchovies, garlic, and chili in a cold skillet and bring up to heat over medium-high heat. Mash the anchovies with a wooden spoon as they cook so they dissolve into a lovely paste—no need to chop them before cooking. As soon as the garlic starts to sizzle, add a ladleful of the pasta water, the broccoli florets, and a generous pinch of salt and pepper. Stir it and cover with a lid. Steam for 10–15 minutes, until the broccoli is completely mushy. Check every now and then to make sure the pan hasn't become too dry. If it does, add another splash of pasta water. Remove from the heat.

Drain the pasta, reserving a cupful of the cooking water. Pour the orecchiette into the skillet containing the mushy broccoli and put back over medium heat. Add a splash of the reserved pasta water and the Parmesan, and toss for 1–2 minutes or until a sauce begins to form and cling to the pasta. Add more of the pasta water, if necessary. Stir through the parsley.

Divide between two bowls, drizzle with a little extra olive oil, grate some extra Parmesan on top, and crack over a few twists of black pepper. Eat immediately.

BUCATINI WITH SPINACH & GARLIC SAUCE

SERVES 4

PREP TIME: 5 MIN * COOK TIME: 12 MIN

V | SoF

14 oz **dried bucatini** or **spaghetti** (we prefer bucatini, because it is more like a chewy noodle)

5 large cloves of **garlic**, thinly sliced

⅓ cup good-quality **extra virgin olive oil**, plus extra for serving

2 (12-oz) pacakages baby **spinach leaves**

a small bunch of **fresh basil leaves**

½ cup **pine nuts**

1 cup freshly grated **Parmesan cheese** (or use **vegetarian Parmesan-style cheese**), plus a little extra for serving

salt and **freshly ground black pepper**

Trust us, you will make this more than once. Sometimes the best things in life are the simplest.

Bring a large pot of heavily salted water to a boil. The water should be as salty as the sea. Add the bucatini or spaghetti and cook for 1 minute less than the package directions.

Meanwhile, put the garlic into a cold skillet with 2 tablespoons of the oil. Heat over medium-high heat and just as the garlic starts to sizzle and become fragrant, add all the spinach. Fry for about 2 minutes until wilted. Remove from the heat.

Scoop out a mugful of the pasta cooking water. Put the spinach, basil leaves, pine nuts, Parmesan, remaining oil, and some pepper into a food processor, along with a splash of the reserved pasta water, and puree into a smooth sauce. If it is too dry and sticky, add a splash more of the pasta water until you are happy with the consistency. It should be like a thick, smooth soup. Transfer the sauce back to the spinach skillet and keep warm over low heat.

When the pasta is ready, drain, reserving another cupful of the cooking water, then transfer the pasta to the spinach pan. Cook for another 1–2 minutes, tossing and stirring continuously, until the sauce starts to cling to the bucatini. If it becomes too thick, add some more pasta water. But equally, it shouldn't be wet—it should have a final consistency where, if you hold a strand of bucatini up in the air, the sauce will stick to it and not slide off.

Transfer to four bowls, drizzle with a little extra olive oi,l and grate a little extra Parmesan over the top. Crack over some black pepper just for good measure. Eat immediately.

SPAGHETTI AGLIO E OLIO

SERVES 4

PREP TIME: 5 MIN * COOK TIME: 12 MIN

DF | V | Ve | NF | SoF

14 oz **dried spaghetti**

8 large cloves of **garlic**, thinly sliced (or add more to taste)

⅔ cup good-quality **extra virgin olive oil**

½ teaspoon **dried red pepper flakes**

juice of ½ **lemon**

a large handful of **fresh parsley**, finely chopped

salt and **freshly ground black pepper**

This is the pasta that Jon Favreau makes for Scarlett Johansson in a famous scene from the movie "Chef." Devastatingly simple. Incredibly tasty. It also just happens to be vegan. Don't be afraid of the amount of garlic. It's the main flavor of the dish and it really needs it.

Bring a large pot of heavily salted water to a boil. The water should be as salty as the sea. Add the spaghetti and cook for 1 minute less than the package directions.

Meanwhile, put the garlic and olive oil into a cold skillet and bring up to heat over medium-high heat. Slowly cook the garlic for about 5 minutes, until softened, fragrant, and just starting to turn golden on the edges. Add the red pepper flakes and a splash of the pasta cooking water to slow down the cooking process. Reduce the heat to low.

When the pasta is ready, drain, reserving a cupful of the cooking water, and transfer the spaghetti to the skillet. Add the lemon juice. Cook for another 1–2 minutes, tossing and stirring constantly until a sauce starts to form and coat the spaghetti. If it starts to dry out, add a splash of the reserved pasta water, but equally it shouldn't be soupy, so cook off any excess liquid. The sauce should be shiny and smooth.

Season to taste with salt and pepper and stir through the parsley. Transfer to four bowls and serve immediately.

PACCHERI WITH SPICED TOMATO SAUCE

SERVES 4

PREP TIME: 5 MIN * COOK TIME: 30–40 MIN

NF | SoF

5 oz **guanciale (Italian cured pork)**, diced

1 **red onion**, diced

3 cloves of **garlic**, thinly sliced

½ teaspoon **dried red pepper flakes**

1 tablespoon **tomato paste**

2 (14½-oz) cans **plum tomatoes**

2 teaspoons **dried oregano**

14 oz **dried paccheri pasta**

a large bunch of **fresh basil leaves**, coarsely chopped (reserving a few small leaves for garnish)

2 oz **Pecorino Romano cheese** (or **Parmesan cheese**, if you can't find Pecorino; ⅔ cup freshly grated)

salt and **freshly ground black pepper**

≡TIP≡

Try to buy the best pasta you can. It's not much more expensive but makes a real difference. Look for "bronze-died" on the package. This means it will have a slightly coarser texture, which helps the sauce to stick.

This is Jack's favorite pasta dish of all time. It comes from the small Italian town of Amatrice, which was tragically devastated by an earthquake in 2016. The paccheri pasta is perfect, because the Amatriciana sauce gets trapped inside to make little sandwiches of deliciousness.

Put the guanciale into a cold skillet and bring up to heat over medium-high heat. You don't need to add any extra oil—enough fat will render out of the guanciale because you started with a cold pan. Cook for 4–5 minutes, until the edges of the meat just start to turn crispy.

Add the onion, garlic, and red pepper flakes and cook, stirring often, for about 8 minutes, until softened. Add the tomato paste and cook for about a minute, stirring constantly with a wooden so it coats the onions, garlic, and guanciale.

Add the canned tomatoes and their juice and crush them with a wooden spoon. Swish out the cans with a splash of water and add to the pan, then add the oregano. Bring to a boil, then reduce the heat to low and simmer, stirring occasionally, for 15–20 minutes, until the sauce thickens. Add salt and pepper to taste.

While the sauce simmers, cook the paccheri in a pot of boiling, heavily salted water for 1 minute less than the package directions. Drain, reserving a cupful of the cooking water. Add the paccheri to the tomato sauce and put the pan over medium heat. Add a splash of the reserved pasta water. Toss and stir constantly for 1–2 minutes, or until the sauce clings to the pasta. Stir through the chopped basil.

Serve in four bowls, grate over the cheese, and top with the reserved basil leaves.

ASPARAGUS CARBONARA

SERVES 4

PREP TIME: 5 MIN * COOK TIME: 15 MIN

NF | SoF

2 golden **egg yolks**

2 cloves of **garlic**, grated

generous 1 cup freshly grated **Pecorino Romano cheese**

12 cranks of **freshly ground black pepper** (we know—it's a lot)

1 lb **dried spaghetti**

6½ oz **guanciale (Italian cured pork)**, cut into ¼-inch cubes

10½ oz **asparagus,** woody ends removed (an easy way to do this is to bend each spear—they will naturally snap where tender), chopped up into 1cm chunks, tips left whole

salt

Oh, how the Italians laugh at how Anglophones cook a carbonara (Jack knows only too well, because he was taught to make this in Italy). There should never be any cream added. The creaminess comes naturally from the emulsion of eggs, Pecorino, and pasta water. This is a healthier twist, because we've added asparagus. If you can't find guanciale, smoked pancetta will work almost as well. Just add a little more black pepper.

In a mixing bowl, whisk together the eggs, garlic, cheese, and pepper. Set aside.

Bring a large pot of heavily salted water to a boil. Add the spaghetti, stir, and cook until al dente (1 minute less than the package directions).

While the pasta is cooking, put the guanciale into a cold skillet and bring up to heat over medium-high heat. You don't need to add any extra oil—enough fat will render out of the guanciale, because you started with a cold pan. Cook for 4–5 minutes, until the edges just start to turn crispy.

Add the asparagus to the crispy guanciale and fry in the fat until softened and nicely charred. Remove from the heat and set aside.

Drain the pasta, reserving a cupful of the cooking water, and then add the pasta to the asparagus-guanciale skillet. Still away from the heat, pour in the egg mixture and toss thoroughly for a couple of minutes, adding the reserved pasta water, a little at a time, if things get too sticky, until the sauce becomes glossy and creamy and coats the back of the spaghetti. The heat of the pasta will cook the eggs.

Transfer to individual bowls and eat immediately.

TROFIE PASTA WITH PESTO & GREEN BEANS

SERVES 2

PREP TIME: 15 MIN ✷ COOK TIME: 10 MIN

V | SoF

⅔ cup **pine nuts**

5 cups **fresh basil leaves**

2 cloves of **garlic**, minced

1 cup freshly grated **Parmesan cheese** (or use **vegetarian Parmesan-style cheese**), plus an extra handful to serve

1 tablespoon **freshly squeezed lemon juice**

about ⅔ cup **extra virgin olive oil**, plus extra for serving (choose one that is not peppery)

9 oz **dried trofie pasta**

1 cup trimmed and halved **green beans**

salt and **freshly ground black pepper**

Trofie comes from Liguria and is the traditional pasta to serve with pesto. If you can't find it, casarecce or rigatoni work well. As for the pesto, it is our version of the traditional Genovese basil pesto. The great thing about pesto is that you can play around with it. Pesto means "paste" in Italian, so you can use any flavor combinations you want. The basic principles stay the same, so use whatever you like the taste of: pistachios and mint; sun-dried tomatoes and almonds; red bell peppers and walnuts.

Heat a dry skillet over medium heat and toast the pine nuts, stirring constantly, for 4–5 minutes, until fragrant. Let cool, then transfer to a food processor.

Add the basil to the food processor and pulse several times. Add the garlic, Parmesan, and lemon juice and pulse again several times. Scrape down the sides with a spatula and pulse again. Start running the food processor and slowly pour in the olive oil until it emulsifies. Add as much as you want, depending on how wet you like your pesto. Taste for seasoning, adjust, and blend again. Spoon into a bowl.

Bring a pot of heavily salted water to a boil and add the pasta. Cook for 1 minute less than the time given on the package. With 3 minutes left, add the green beans. Drain the pasta and green beans, reserving one cupful of the cooking water.

Put everything back into the pot away from the heat. Stir in the pesto (keep in mind you probably won't need it all—just enough to coat everything). If the mixture is a little thick, add a splash of the reserved pasta water a little at a time. Keep stirring for a minute or so until everything has emulsified and the pesto clings to the pasta.

Serve in two bowls, sprinkle with the extra Parmesan, and drizzle a little olive oil over the top. Crack over some black pepper and eat immediately.

FRESH TAGLIATELLE
WITH ZUCCHINI & HERBED PANGRATTATO

SERVES 4

PREP TIME: 10 MIN * COOK TIME: 20–25 MIN

NF | SoF

⅓ cup **extra virgin olive oil**

¾ loaf of **stale bread**, such as **ciabatta** or a small **sourdough**, crusts removed, processed or chopped finely into bread crumbs

1 teaspoon **salt**

8 twists of **freshly ground black pepper**

4 sprigs of **fresh rosemary**, leaves picked and finely chopped

zest of 1 **unwaxed lemon**

5 **canned anchovy fillets**, drained

4 large cloves of **garlic**, thinly sliced

2 **zucchini**, halved lengthwise and cut into ¼-inch-thick semicircles

1¼ cups **crème fraîche**

a squeeze of **lemon juice**

1 lb **fresh tagliatelle**

a handful of **fresh mint leaves**, chopped

salt and **freshly ground black pepper**

Pangrattato is Italian for "bread crumbs." They add a depth of flavor to pasta and were used as an alternative for Parmesan cheese by Italians who couldn't afford the cheese, so they make a great substitute for anyone who avoids regular Parmesan. Here, they add texture to creamy zucchini and crème fraîche.

Heat ¼ cup of the olive oil in a large skillet, add the bread crumbs, measured salt and pepper, and the rosemary and cook for 5 minutes or until golden brown. Stir through the lemon zest, then set aside in a bowl.

Wipe out the skillet, then heat the remaining 2 tablespoons of olive oil over medium-high heat and add the anchovies. Cook for 2 minutes, until they start to break up. Add the garlic and cook for another minute. Finally, add the zucchini and fry for another 8–10 minutes, until tender and soft.

Stir in the crème fraîche, mix thoroughly, add the lemon juice, taste for seasoning and adjust, if necessary, then reduce the heat.

Bring a large pot of heavily salted water to a boil. The water should be as salty as the sea. Add the tagliatelle and cook for about 2 minutes or according to the package directions. Drain, reserving a cupful of the cooking water, then add the pasta to the skillet. Cook for another 1–2 minutes, mixing constantly, until the sauce starts to bind to the pasta, forming a thick, glossy coating. Use a little of the reserved pasta water, if it needs loosening, but be sparing. Stir through the mint, reserving a little to serve. Transfer to four bowls and top each with a generous amount of the pangrattato and a sprinkling of mint.

KENTUCKY FRIED CAULIFLOWER

SERVES 4

PREP TIME: 15 MIN, PLUS CHILLING * COOK TIME: 20 MIN

V | Ve | NF

1 teaspoon **salt**

1 teaspoon **freshly ground black pepper**

1 teaspoon **celery salt**

1 teaspoon **medium chili powder**

1 teaspoon **sweet paprika**

1 teaspoon **smoked paprika**

1 teaspoon **ground cumin**

1 teaspoon **garlic powder**

1 teaspoon **onion powder**

1 teaspoon **dried sage**

1 teaspoon **dried oregano**

1⅔ cups **dairy-free milk** (we use **soy milk** but **oat milk** also works well)

2 tablespoons **apple cider vinegar** (Ve if needed)

2 tablespoons **hot sauce** (we like Frank's the best and it is easy to find)

1 large **cauliflower**, cut into large florets, about 1¼ inches in size

2 tablespoons **cornstarch**

2 cups **all-purpose flour**

vegetable oil

pickles and your favorite **dipping sauce**, to serve

This is a properly tasty vegan alternative to fried chicken.

In a small bowl, combine all the seasonings and dried herbs and mix well with a fork.

In a large bowl, whisk together the soy milk, apple cider vinegar, and hot sauce (this will create a vegan buttermilk). Add half the spice mix and whisk until smooth. Add the cauliflower florets and mix well with your hands until they are well coated. Cover and refrigerate for at least 1 hour.

In another large bowl, mix the remaining half of the spice mix with the cornstarch and all-purpose flour. Set aside.

Remove the cauliflower from the refrigerator. Dip each floret in the seasoned flour and place on a tray. When all have been coated thoroughly, repeat the process but this time dip each floret in the "buttermilk" mixture, turning to coat, and then again in the seasoned flour.

In a large, deep, heavy saucepan, heat about 2½ inches of vegetable oil over medium heat until it reaches 350°F, or until a cube of day-old bread fizzles and browns in 30 seconds. (If the oil is too hot, the batter will burn; if it's too cold, the batter will be soggy.)

Fry the cauliflower florets, in batches, for 5–6 minutes, until golden brown and crispy. Remove from the oil using tongs or a slotted spoon and transfer to a wire rack or paper towels to cool and for the excess oil to drain off. Let the oil come back up to temperature between each batch, and repeat until all the florets are cooked.

Serve with pickles and your favorite dipping sauce.

LEON JACK WINGS

2½ tablespoons **vegetable oil**, plus extra for pan-frying

⅓ cup **all-purpose flour**

1 cup **plant-based milk** (NF, SoF if needed), warmed

¼ teaspoon **Marmite**

1 teaspoon **sweet smoked paprika**

½ teaspoon **garlic powder**

3 tablespoons finely grated **vegan Parmesan-style cheese**

½ teaspoon **vegetable bouillon powder**

a pinch of **freshly grated nutmeg**

1½ tablespoons **soy sauce**

3 cups drained **canned unripe jackfruit** (about 2 cans), rinsed and well-shredded (fish out any hard pieces of jellylike seeds)

2 cups **store-bought bread crumbs**

⅓ cup **cornstarch**

salt (optional)

your choice of **mayo** or **sauces**—try **Aioli Mayo** or **Thom's BBQ Sauce** (either can be Ve, see pages 188 and 191), or **ketchup**, to serve

Jackfruit, when unripe and shredded, makes a mind-blowing vegan substitute for chicken or pork. In 2019, we launched our popular jack wings: crispy coated, cheesy jackfruit nuggets of joy. They're not wings, obviously, but they're still delicious.

Heat the oil in a large saucepan over medium heat. When hot, add the flour and cook, stirring, until you have a smooth, pale gold paste. Add a splash of the milk and cook, stirring, until combined. Add the rest of the milk gradually until you have a thick white sauce. Reduce the heat to low and continue to cook, stirring constantly, for 6–8 minutes, until smooth, thick, and almost stretchy. Add the Marmite, smoked paprika, garlic powder, vegan cheese, vegetable bouillon powder, nutmeg, and soy sauce. Stir well, then taste for seasoning.

Mix the jackfruit and white sauce well. Taste again—it should be meaty and savory. Put the mixture in the refrigerator, covered, to chill for an hour or overnight.

When ready to cook, mix together the bread crumbs and cornstarch in a wide bowl. Set a wide saucepan over medium heat and generously cover the bottom of the pan with oil. Remove the jackfruit mixture from the refrigerator and fry a little for a minute or two, then taste to check the seasoning and correct, if needed.

Shape the jackfruit mixture into nuggets, then roll them in the bread crumbs, coating thoroughly. Pan-fry 6–8 nuggets for about 2 minutes on each side, moving them gently so they don't lose their shape. When cooked on all sides, crisp, and a rich dark golden brown, remove from the pan using tongs. Drain on a plate lined with paper towels and keep warm while you cook the rest in the same way.

Eat hot, with sauces for dunking.

=TIP=

This is also good with flash-fried rare steak, cut into strips; pan-fried fish fillets, such as mackerel or bass; or Crispy Tofu (see page 145). Leftover sauce will keep in a sealed bottle or jar in the refrigerator for up to a week or two.

CHICKEN DONBURI

SERVES 4

PREP TIME: 15 MIN ＊ COOK TIME: 20 MIN

WF | GF | DF | NF

2 cups **glutinous rice**, rinsed

2 **eggs**, lightly beaten

2 cups **panko** or **gluten-free bread crumbs**

all-purpose flour (WF, GF if needed)

neutral cooking oil

4 skinless, boneless **chicken breasts**, cut into ½-inch slices across the grain

3½ oz **fresh mushrooms**, ideally **shiitake or oyster**, sliced or torn if large

salt and **freshly ground black pepper**

FOR THE SAUCE:

2 tablespoons **mirin**

¼ cup **soy sauce** (WF, GF if needed)

a pinch of **superfine sugar**

salt and **freshly ground black pepper**

TO SERVE:

⅛ **green cabbage**, shredded

1 large **carrot**, peeled and julienned into thin matchsticks or ribbons

3 **scallions**, sliced thinly on an angle

black or **white sesame seeds**, or a mixture

Donburi are fast-food dishes served in Japan, usually in bowls with meat, fish, tofu, or vegetables over rice and a soy-base sauce. This is Rebecca's completely nontraditional take on it, which she makes at home.

Bring the rice and 2 cups cold water to a boil, then turn down to a simmer, cover, and cook for 12 minutes. Remove from the heat and let steam, covered.

Fill one bowl with the beaten eggs, another with half the bread crumbs, and another with 3–4 tablespoons of flour seasoned with salt and pepper.

Put a large, wide skillet over medium heat and add about ¼ inch of oil. Taking half the chicken pieces, dip each into the flour, then the egg and followed by the bread crumbs, making sure they are completely covered with a layer of each. Put the coated chicken into the pan and cook until golden brown on the bottom, then turn and cook until golden all over and cooked through—about 5 minutes in total. If the bread crumbs start to burn, turn down the heat. Put the cooked chicken onto a plate lined with paper towels and keep warm. Repeat with the rest of the pieces, adding more bread crumbs or flour to the bowls as needed.

While the chicken cooks, pour the sauce ingredients into a small saucepan with scant ½ cup of water, season to taste, and warm through.

When all the chicken is cooked, increase the heat, scooping out any burned crumbs, and stir-fry the mushrooms quickly. (You can also briefly scramble any leftover egg wash and add it to the finished donburi, too, if you want.)

Divide the rice, chicken, cabbage, and carrot among four bowls and spoon some of the sauce over the top. Sprinkle with the scallions and sesame seeds to serve.

BIAN DANG

SERVES 2

PREP TIME: 25 MIN, PLUS OPTIONAL MARINATING ∗ COOK TIME: 30 MIN

WF | GF | DF | NF

3 tablespoons **soy sauce** (WF, GF if needed)

1 teaspoon **Chinese five-spice**

2 teaspoons **superfine sugar**

1 clove of **garlic**, crushed

2 teaspoons **Chinese rice wine** (optional)

2 **free-range pork chops** (cut through the fatty zest at ¾-inch intervals), pounded to about ½ inch thick

vegetable oil

cornstarch, for dredging

salt

FOR THE QUICK TEA EGGS:

2 **eggs**, at room temperature

1 **black tea bag**

2 tablespoons **soy sauce** (WF, GF if needed), plus extra to serve (optional)

1 teaspoon **Chinese five-spice**

1 **bay leaf**

1 teaspoon **superfine sugar**

a generous pinch of **salt**

TO SERVE:

⅔ cup **Thai jasmine rice**

7 oz **mustardy Asian greens (choy sum** or, if possible, **water spinach)**, chopped

This is a highly—heretically—Anglicized version of the original dish served in boxes on trains in Taiwan. But it's delicious. And we hope Taiwan forgives us.

In a large wide container, mix together the soy sauce, five-spice, sugar, garlic, rice wine, and a generous pinch of salt. Add the chops and rub the marinade into the meat. Cover and refrigerate for a couple of hours, if possible.

For the quick tea eggs, have ready a bowl of iced water. Bring a saucepan of water to a boil and add the eggs. Reduce the heat to medium and cook for 7 minutes, then put the eggs into the iced water to cool. Meanwhile, put the remaining tea egg ingredients with ⅔ cup of water into a small saucepan and bring to a boil. Remove from the heat and let cool. Carefully peel the cooled eggs and keep in the cooled tea mixture, turning now and then, until ready to serve.

About 20 minutes before you want to serve, put the rice into a saucepan with 1⅓ cups of cold water and a pinch of salt. Put over medium heat, bring to a simmer, then cover with a lid and cook for 12 minutes. Remove from the heat and let stand, still covered, for 5 minutes or so.

Fill a saucepan with salted boiling water, bring back to a boil, then add the Asian greens. Blanch for 1 minute, then drain and set aside. Keep warm.

Put a wide skillet over medium heat and add about ½ inch of vegetable oil. Spread some cornstarch onto a plate. Coat each flattened chop in the cornstarch, then carefully lower into the pan. Cook for 2 minutes on each side or until deep brown on the outside and no longer pink within. Remove and drain briefly on paper towels.

Remove the eggs from their marinade and serve the rice, greens, chops, and eggs with a little extra soy sauce, if you want.

CHICKEN, CHORIZO & SHRIMP JAMBALAYA

SERVES 4

PREP TIME: 15 MIN * COOK TIME: 55 MIN

WF | GF | DF | NF | SoF

1 tablespoon **olive oil**

4 skin-on, boneless **chicken thighs**

3½ oz **chorizo**, sliced

1 **onion**, diced

1 **red bell pepper**, seeded and thinly sliced

1 **celery stalk**, diced

4 cloves of **garlic**, crushed

1 **red chili,** seeded and thinly sliced

1 teaspoon **cayenne pepper**

1 teaspoon **paprika**

1 teaspoon **dried thyme**

1 teaspoon **dried oregano**

1 teaspoon **freshly ground black pepper**

scant ½ cup **dry white wine**

1⅓ cups **long-grain white rice**

1 (14½-oz) can **diced tomatoes**

about 2 cups hot **chicken broth** (you may need slightly more, depending on how long the rice takes to cook)

a hefty pinch of **saffron threads**

2 **bay leaves**

12 **raw jumbo shrimp**, peeled and deveined

a large handful of **fresh parsley**, coarsely chopped

salt

Donald Gunn is the father of Jack's roommate, Henry. He also happens to be an incredible home cook and, while living and working in the United States, developed and wrote down a bunch of delicious traditional recipes. He kindly wrote out, laminated, and sent Jack his now-no-longer-secret jambalaya recipe to be used in this book. Thank you, Donald.

Heat the oil in a large, heavy, deep saucepan with a lid (such as a Dutch oven). When it is shimmering, add the chicken thighs, skin side down. Season with a pinch of salt. Brown the meat for 5–6 minutes, and then flip over and brown for another 2–3 minutes. Remove from the pan, coarsely chop, and put into a bowl.

Without wiping the pan, brown the chorizo for 5–6 minutes. Remove and add to the chicken bowl.

Again without wiping the pan, add the onion, red bell pepper, and celery. Cook for 5 minutes, stirring often. Add the garlic, chili, cayenne pepper, paprika, thyme, oregano, and black pepper. Cook for another 3 minutes, stirring now and then.

Add the white wine and deglaze the bottom of the pan, scraping off any brown sediment, then let simmer for 1–2 minutes. Add the chicken and chorizo back in, along with the rice, tomatoes, broth, saffron, and bay leaves.

Cover and simmer for 20 minutes. Stir through the shrimp, then cover again and cook for another 8–10 minutes, until the rice is tender and the shrimp are pink and opaque. Double-check a piece of chicken to see if the meat is done and the juices run clear. If it is getting dry and the rice has absorbed all the liquid before it has finished cooking, add some more hot broth.

Add salt and pepper to taste, stir through the parsley, and serve immediately.

POKE

SERVES 4

PREP TIME: 15 MIN ✳ COOK TIME: 12 MIN, PLUS STANDING

WF | GF | DF | NF

2 cups **sushi rice**, rinsed

1 tablespoon **rice vinegar** (optional)

a pinch of **salt**

½ teaspoon **superfine sugar** (optional), plus an extra pinch

1 tablespoon **dried hijiki seaweed**

1 tablespoon **dried wakame seaweed**

2 tablespoons **soy sauce** (WF, GF if needed)

2 teaspoons **sesame oil**

2 teaspoons **mirin**

10 oz **very fresh sushi-grade tuna fillet** (or any **sushi-grade fish fillet**), chopped into ¾-inch cubes

1 ripe **avocado**, peeled, pitted, and diced (see page 87 for the dicing technique)

16 slices of **cucumber**

3 **scallions**, finely chopped on an angle

¼ cup **crispy fried onions** (from a package, or make your own, see page 89)

black or **white sesame seeds**, to garnish

Poke is a Hawaiian unwrapped, sushi-style, fast-food dish. It is usually made with raw fish, although we included a recipe for beet poke in our "Fast Vegan" book. You could add finely sliced raw vegetables, such as red cabbage, radish, or broccoli, to this version, or cooked edamame (soybeans) or cubes of cooked squash. Feel free to drizzle with kewpie mayo, Sriracha sauce, or more soy sauce. If raw fish isn't your thing, it's just as good with cooked white fish, salmon, or shrimp. The two dried seaweeds are easy to find online, as well as in some large grocery stores and in Chinese or Japanese grocers.

Bring the rice and 2½ cups of cold water to a boil, then turn down to a simmer, cover, and cook for 12 minutes. Remove from the heat and let steam, covered, for 20 minutes. Stir in the rice vinegar, if using, salt and ½ teaspoon of sugar, if using, and fluff up with a fork. If not serving warm immediately, chill in the refrigerator until ready to serve, or set aside while you make the rest of the dish.

Put the dried seaweeds into a small bowl and pour over enough boiling water to just cover them. Let stand for 5 minutes to rehydrate, then drain.

Mix together the soy sauce, sesame oil, mirin, and the remaining pinch of sugar, and pour into a bowl with the tuna, avocado, and rehydrated seaweed. Toss gently.

Divide the cooked rice among four bowls. Top the rice with the tuna mixture, then arrange the cucumber next to it. Sprinkle with the scallions and crispy fried onions and garnish with the sesame seeds. Eat immediately.

CRISPY TOFU WITH BLACK RICE

SERVES 4

PREP TIME: 15 MIN * COOK TIME: 45 MIN

DF | V | Ve

a pinch of **salt**

1⅓ cups **black rice** (or ordinary **long-grain white rice**)

1½ tablespoons **vegetable oil**

1 heaping tablespoon **cornstarch**

10 oz **extra-firm tofu**, pressed to remove excess liquid then cut into ½-inch cubes

1⅓ cups **frozen edamame (soybeans)**

1¾ cups sliced **broccoli**

2 cups diagonnaly sliced **green beans**

3 tablespoons **cashew nuts** or **peanuts**, coarsely chopped

3 **scallions**, cut into 1cm slices on an angle

⅓ **cucumber**, sliced into ribbons

black or **white sesame seeds** (or a mixture), to serve

FOR THE DRESSING:

1 tablespoon **soy sauce**

1–2 tablespoons **freshly squeezed lime juice**, or to taste

1 tablespoon **sesame oil**

3 tablespoons good-quality **mayonnaise** (Ve if needed)

Black rice takes a little longer to cook than white rice, but is so tasty (and nutrient-dense) that it's worth the wait. If you want to add more to your bowl, try finely sliced carrot, diced avocado, fresh or pickled ginger, sliced radishes, corn, or even marinated Quick Tea Eggs (see page 138).

Bring 4 cups of water up to a boil in a saucepan and add the salt. Add the rice and simmer for 30–45 minutes (black rice can be variable in its cook time), until tender but with some bite.

Toward the end of the cooking time, start cooking the tofu. Put a large, wide skillet over medium heat and add the oil. Put the cornstarch into a bowl and add the tofu. Toss gently, using your hands, to coat each piece lightly. Add the tofu cubes to the pan and cook for about 2 minutes on each side, until golden and crisp all over.

While the tofu is crisping up, prepare the rest of the vegetables. Put the edamame, broccoli, and green beans into a separate saucepan of boiling water and bring back to a boil. Cook for 2 minutes, so the vegetables remain crisp. Drain and set aside.

Make the dressing by whisking together all the ingredients in a small bowl, then gradually add just enough water to make it thin enough to pour—probably only a tablespoon or so.

When the rice is done, drain it thoroughly. Divide among four bowls, then arrange the vegetables on top on one side. Remove the tofu from the pan and divide among the bowls. Add the nuts to the skillet over medium heat, tossing them for just a minute or so, to lightly toast, then add them to the bowls, along with the scallions and cucumber. Pour over the dressing, then top each bowl with a pinch of sesame seeds and serve.

GRILLED & BAKED

FISH KABOBS WITH CUCUMBER RAITA

SERVES 6–8

PREP TIME: 10 MIN, PLUS MARINATING * COOK TIME: 10 MIN

WF | GF | NF | SoF

FOR THE CUCUMBER RAITA:

1 small **cucumber**, grated

1²⁄₃ cups **Greek yogurt**

2 cloves of **garlic**, grated

¼ cup finely chopped **fresh dill**

zest and juice of ½ **unwaxed lemon**

½ teaspoon **ground cumin**

salt and **freshly ground black pepper**

FOR THE SKEWERS:

⅓ cup **extra virgin olive oil**, plus extra for
    greasing and drizzling

2 cloves of **garlic**, crushed or grated

zest and juice of 1 **unwaxed lemon**

2 teaspoons finely chopped **fresh
    rosemary leaves**

1½ teaspoons **salt**

½ teaspoon **freshly ground black pepper**

½ teaspoon **ground cumin**

½ teaspoon **ground turmeric**

¼ teaspoon **dried red pepper flakes**

1½ lb firm **white fish fillets**, such as cod or
    halibut

6–8 long, woody **rosemary stems**, leaves
    removed, or **wooden/bamboo skewers**

a small bunch of **fresh parsley leaves**,
    chopped, to garnish

Simple and delicious, these make us think of barbecues on a late summer evening. The rosemary skewers are optional—you could just use regular wooden/bamboo ones—but they add a lovely background flavor and look really cool on the plate, too.

If you're using wooden or bamboo skewers, soak them in water for 20 minutes before using.

To make the raita, squeeze the water out of the grated cucumber, then combine in a bowl with the yogurt, garlic, dill, lemon zest and juice, cumin, and seasoning to taste. Cover and refrigerate.

For the kabobs, in a large bowl, mix together the oil, garlic, lemon zest and juice, chopped rosemary, salt, pepper, cumin, turmeric, and red pepper flakes.

Cut the fish into cubes, about 1½ inches in size, then put them into the marinade. Mix thoroughly with your hands, making sure every piece of fish is coated, then cover and refrigerate for at least 30 minutes. (However, do not leave it for longer than 2 hours or the fish will start to break down.)

When ready to cook, thread the rosemary (or wooden/bamboo) skewers through the marinated fish cubes.

Cook the skewers on a heated and oiled barbecue grill (or hot broiler pan), turning once, for about 10 minutes, until the edges are lightly browned and the fish is cooked through.

Put the kabobs onto a platter and sprinkle with the chopped parsley to garnish, drizzle a little extra olive oil over the top, and serve with the cucumber raita.

SUYA

SERVES 4

PREP TIME: 10 MIN, PLUS CHILLING * COOK TIME: 7–8 MIN

WF | GF | DF | SoF

1⅓ cups **roasted peanuts**

5 cloves of **garlic**, crushed or grated

2 teaspoons **ground ginger**

2 **beef bouillon cubes**, crumbled up between your fingers (WF, GF if needed)

1 teaspoon **salt**

2 teaspoons **freshly ground black pepper**

2 teaspoons **onion powder**

2 teaspoons **smoked paprika**

1 teaspoon **dried chipotle flakes**, crushed or finely chopped

½ teaspoon **cayenne pepper**

2¼ lb **tenderloin steak**, trimmed of any fat

10–12 **wooden/bamboo skewers** (soaked in water for 20 minutes before use)

vegetable oil, for brushing

Grilled meat skewers are a common street-food dish in West Africa. This recipe is our version of suya, Nigerian beef skewers rolled in a spiced peanut crumb, although the crumb is also delicious around chicken or fish. They taste best cooked over charcoal, but a hot broiler pan will do the job.

Pulse the roasted peanuts in a food processor until they are like coarse bread crumbs—but be careful not to go so far that you have a paste.

Add the garlic, ginger, bouillon cubes, salt, pepper, onion powder, smoked paprika, chipotle flakes, and cayenne pepper. Pulse to combine, but don't overblend.

Cut the steak into long, thick strips about 1½ inches thick and wide. Thread the pieces of beef onto the skewers with each skewer running lengthwise through the meat (like a corn dog).

Brush the meat with some oil, then press the peanut mixture firmly onto each beef skewer, making sure you coat it completely. Put onto a plate, cover, and refrigerate for at least 2 hours.

Heat a barbecue grill or broiler to high. Oil the grill grate or broiler rack, then cook the skewers for 7–8 minutes, until golden and crusty on the outside and pink in the middle, turning once. Don't move them around too often or too early, because otherwise you will knock the coating off.

Remove from the heat, let rest for 2 minutes, then dig in.

YAKITORI MUSHROOMS

SERVES 6

PREP TIME: 10 MIN * COOK TIME: 25–30 MIN

WF | GF | DF | V | Ve | NF

FOR THE GLAZE:

½ cup **soy sauce** (WF, GF if needed)

½ cup **mirin**

¼ cup **sake** (or **dry sherry** if you can't find sake)

1 tablespoon grated **fresh ginger**

2 large cloves of **garlic**, grated

2 tablespoons packed **light brown sugar**

FOR THE SKEWERS:

8 **scallions**, dark green tips reserved, the rest cut into 2½-inch sticks

6 **bamboo/wooden skewers**, soaked for 20 minutes in water

18 large fresh **shiitake mushrooms**

vegetable oil, for brushing

⅓ cup **white sesame seeds**, to serve

Yakitori are incredibly popular in Japan. They are traditionally made with chicken, but this vegetarian alternative packs just as much flavor, thanks to the meaty mushrooms and delicious teriyaki-like glaze. Although best grilled on a barbecue, they can also be cooked in a nonstick skillet on the stove.

It's important the mushrooms aren't too small, otherwise they will be difficult to skewer and shrink to nothingness on the grill. Portobello mushrooms work nicely, too, but may be a little on the large side, so cut them in half if so.

For the glaze, whisk together the soy sauce, mirin, and sake in a saucepan over medium heat. Add the ginger, garlic, sugar, and two of the reserved dark green scallion tips. Bring to a simmer, then reduce the heat and cook, stirring regularly, for 15–18 minutes, until the sauce is thick and glossy.

Thread a skewer lengthwise through a mushroom, then widthwise through a piece of scallion, then another mushroom, another scallion, continuing to fill each skewer.

Heat a barbecue grill or broiler to high. Brush both the grate or rack and the skewers with oil, then put the skewers on the grill or in the pan. Brush them with the glaze using a pastry brush as they cook, turning every now and then. The mushrooms and onions should turn a deep, dark golden brown in 10–15 minutes.

While the skewers are cooking, toast the sesame seeds in a hot, dry skillet for a few minutes until golden, then remove from the heat and transfer to a small bowl.

Transfer the skewers to a platter, brush once again with the remaining glaze, and sprinkle with the toasted sesame seeds to serve.

GARLICKY SHRIMP

SERVES 6

PREP TIME: 5 MIN * COOK TIME: 5 MIN

WF | GF | NF | SoF

4 tablespoons **unsalted butter**

2 tablespoons **olive oil**

4 large cloves of **garlic**, minced

1 small **shallot**, minced

1 teaspoon **dried oregano**

¼ teaspoon **dried red pepper flakes**

a pinch of **cayenne pepper**

1 teaspoon **caper preserving liquid**
   (optional, but adds a lovely tang)

zest and juice of 1 **unwaxed lemon**

1 lb 10 oz **raw jumbo shrimp**, peeled
   and deveined

handful of **fresh parsley leaves**

salt and **freshly ground black pepper**

So simple, so tasty. This works best on a barbecue grill, because of the smoky flavor, but you can use this butter mix to cook the shrimp in the oven or in a pan, if you prefer. As Bubba tells Forrest Gump, "Shrimp is the fruit of the sea. You can barbecue it, boil it, broil it, bake it, sauté it."

Heat the barbecue grill or broiler to medium-high.

Heat the butter with the oil in a small saucepan over medium heat until the butter melts, then add the garlic, shallot, oregano, red pepper flakes, cayenne pepper, caper preserving liquid, if using, and lemon juice. Cook for 1 minute until fragrant, taste and adjust the seasoning, taste again, and then remove from the heat. (If it starts to solidify before you start cooking the shrimp, heat gently until liquid again.)

Lay out the shrimp on the grate or rack (or a medium-hot grill pan if grilling on the stove), then grill until golden and pink, brushing often with the garlic butter, and turning them once. They will need 2–3 minutes per side.

Transfer to a plate, brush again with any remaining garlic butter, and sprinkle with the lemon zest and parsley. Dig in.

=TIP=

If you want to make it easier to turn the shrimp, thread them onto wooden/bamboo skewers that have been soaked in water for 20 minutes.

≡TIP≡

You can store any leftover (unused) sauce in a scrupulously clean jar or bottle with a lid in the refrigerator for up to a week.

PIRI PIRI ANYTHING

SERVES 4–6

PREP TIME: 10 MIN, PLUS MARINATING * COOK TIME: 20–25 MIN

WF | GF | NF

4–8 skin-on, bone-in **chicken thighs** or
   4 whole **chicken legs** or 20 **chicken wings**
or 14 oz extra-firm **tofu**, pressed to
   remove excess liquid (plus 1 tablespoon
   cornstarch)
or 1–2 lb prepped **vegetables**, for roasting
vegetable oil, for greasing

FOR THE PIRI PIRI SPICE SAUCE:
3 cloves of **garlic**, coarsely chopped
¼ cup **white wine vinegar**
2 **hot red chilies**, seeded
1–2 small, **Thai bird's eye** or **piri piri
   chilies**, seeded
5–6 (or more, to taste—we find the sauce
   mellows as it cooks) small **dried red
   chilies**, crumbled
1 **red bell pepper**, seeded and coarsely
   chopped
1 teaspoon **smoked paprika**
⅓ cup **olive oil**
2½ teaspoons **fine salt**
1 teaspoon **freshly squeezed lemon juice**
¼ teaspoon **hot piri piri powder** or **hot
   chili powder**
1 teaspoon **whiskey** (optional)

This is HOT. In all the ways.

For the piri piri sauce, blend all the ingredients in a blender until smooth.

For piri piri chicken: Toss the chicken in 3–4 tablespoons of the sauce in a bowl. Cover and refrigerate for up to 2 hours. Heat the oven to 400°F. Put the chicken in a large greased baking pan and roast for 15 minutes for large pieces or 10 minutes for wings. Remove from the oven, baste, and drizzle with some more piri piri sauce. Return to the oven to finish cooking: legs will need a total of up to 55 minutes, thighs 35–40 minutes, and wings about 20 minutes. The chicken is done when the skin is golden and glazed with sticky marinade and when the meat is pierced to the bone, the juices run clear.

For piri piri tofu: Add the cornstarch to ¼ cup of sauce, then toss the tofu in the mixture (14 oz is enough for 4 people). Cover and refrigerate for an hour. Put a lightly oiled, wide heavy skillet over low heat and fry the tofu gently on all sides, turning as soon as it's golden and no longer sticking to the pan. When cooked, taste and check for salt (because tofu is bland to start with).

For piri piri roasted vegetables: Heat the oven to 400°F. Depending on the size and firmness of the veggies, cook them a little in the oven before adding the sauce. Ideally, the sauce will have about 15 minutes in the oven, so work backward. Sweet potato slices will need up to 30 minutes, whereas zucchini, bell pepper, and eggplant chunks or slices will probably need only 20 minutes. When partly cooked, coat the vegetable pieces in the piri piri sauce, return to the oven in a roasting pan, and cook until the cut edges begin to turn golden and the vegetables are tender but not mushy. Serve immediately.

DENAI'S VEGAN JAMAICAN PATTIES

MAKES 12

PREP TIME: 25 MIN, PLUS RESTING, COOLING & CHILLING * COOK TIME: 1 HOUR 5 MIN

DF | V | Ve

FOR THE DOUGH:

3⅔ cups **white spelt flour**, plus extra
   to dust

1½ teaspoons **fine salt**

2 tablespoons **ground turmeric**

12 oz (1½ cups) cold **vegan block butter**,
   cubed, plus 5 tablespoons melted
   and cooled

up to ½ cup **iced water**

2 tablespoons **plant-based milk**

1 tablespoon **maple syrup**

FOR THE FILLING:

2 tablespoons **coconut oil**

1 **red onion**, diced

1 teaspoon **ground allspice**

1 tablespoon picked **fresh thyme leaves**

3 cloves of **garlic**, finely chopped

½ **Scotch bonnet chili,** seeded and
   minced (you might want to use gloves or
   use a milder chili if you don't like heat)

1 teaspoon **tamari** or **soy sauce**

2 **roasted peppers** from a jar, seeded and
   diced

3 **scallions**, finely chopped

1⅔ cups really good-quality **coconut milk**

1 large **sweet potato,** peeled and cut into
   ½-inch cubes

salt and **freshly ground black pepper**

Our friend, British-Jamaican musician and chef Denai Moore, started her London restaurant Dee's Table after a particularly inspiring visit to Jamaica. There, patties are an easy-to-find street food, but it's not so easy to find a vegan version, so Denai created this recipe. (You'll also find plantain gnocchi and mango lime curd tart when you visit her restaurant.)

For the dough, sift the flour into a food processor and add the salt and turmeric. Pulse until completely combined. With the food processor on its slowest setting, slowly drop the butter cubes into the mixture until the consistency is like fine bread crumbs. Add the iced water slowly, with the machine still running, until the dough combines into a rough ball (you may not need all the water).

Lightly flour a clean work surface (or a large board, if your countertop is white) and tip out the dough, then quickly form it into two balls (you don't want to work the dough at this point, because your hands may melt the butter). Wrap the dough in plastic wrap and let it rest in the refrigerator for at least an hour or until firm.

Melt the coconut oil in a large saucepan with a lid over medium heat. Add the onion and a pinch of salt and sauté for 8–10 minutes, until fragrant and translucent. Now add the seasonings: the allspice, thyme, garlic, Scotch bonnet, and tamari or soy sauce, cooking over slightly lower heat for another minute so all the flavors can come together.

Add the roasted peppers and scallions, stir for 30 seconds, then add the coconut milk and bring to a simmer. Add the sweet potato and mix well, then cover and cook over low heat until the sweet potato is tender. When the sweet potato is cooked through, check and adjust the seasoning with salt and pepper. Let the mixture cool in a bowl while the dough continues to rest.

When ready to assemble, heat the oven to 400°F. Line two baking pans with parchment paper.

Take the rested dough out of the refrigerator, cut each ball in half, and then cut each half into three pieces, forming 12 pieces of dough. Lightly flour the work surface again, and roll out a ball of dough to about ¼ inch thick. Using a small bowl or pastry cutter, about 8¼ inches across, and a sharp knife, cut out the dough to make a perfect circle. (Discard the scraps. Unfortunately, if you reroll the excess dough, you will have misshapen patties, so it's not really worth it.)

Put 3 tablespoons of the cooled, melted butter into a small bowl, then use a little to brush each disk. Put a heaping tablespoon of the filling on one half of the pastry circle, slightly flattening out the filling and leaving about ½ inch space around the rim.

Fold the other half over the filling and press the two layers of dough together using a fork and your fingers around the edge.

Place the patty on a lined baking pan, and repeat until all of the patties are made. Chill the pan in the freezer for 15 minutes so the dough will be extra cold when it hits the oven (for extra flaky patties).

Prick each chilled patty with a fork a few times on top to allow for steam to escape. Mix the milk, maple syrup, and remaining 2 tablespoons of melted butter together and brush each patty with this mixture. Bake for 20 minutes, until golden. Remove from the oven and cool slightly before serving— they will be piping hot inside.

═TIP═

This recipe uses roasted peppers in a jar as a shortcut, but if you have more time, try charring raw bell peppers over a gas burner on the stove.

OVEN-BAKED BUTTERMILK "FRIED" CHICKEN

SERVES 4

PREP TIME: 10 MIN, PLUS MARINATING ∗ COOK TIME: 30 MIN

NF | SoF

scant 1 cup **buttermilk**

juice of ½ **lemon**

1 teaspoon **salt**

1 teaspoon **sweet smoked paprika**

½ teaspoon **freshly ground black pepper**

½ teaspoon **garlic powder**

½ teaspoon **onion powder**

¼ teaspoon **cayenne pepper**

8 large skinless, boneless **chicken thighs**

FOR THE COATING:

1½ cups **panko bread crumbs**

1 teaspoon **salt**

1 teaspoon **dried parsley**

1 teaspoon **dried oregano**

1 teaspoon **smoked sweet paprika**

1 teaspoon **freshly ground black pepper**

1 teaspoon **onion powder**

1 teaspoon **garlic powder**

½ teaspoon **cayenne pepper**

Many buttermilk chicken dishes are deep-fried, but this is a tasty, healthy way to get that fried chicken flavor without all the oil. Make sure the oven is screaming hot to get a crispy coating. Serve with Avocado and Butter Lettuce salad (see page 87), any of the slaws on pages 95–97, Crispy Baked Fries (page 173), or Chickpea Panisse (page 182) and Aioli Mayo (page 188).

Whisk together the buttermilk, lemon juice, salt, smoked paprika, black pepper, garlic powder, onion powder, and cayenne pepper in a bowl. Put the chicken thighs into the marinade, turn until coated all over, then cover and refrigerate for a minimum of 4 hours, ideally overnight.

Heat the oven to 425°F. Line a baking pan with parchment paper.

For the coating, combine all the ingredients in a shallow bowl, mixing well. Remove the chicken thighs from the marinade, one at a time, and dredge in the bread crumb mix to coat all over. Place on the lined baking pan.

Bake for 25–30 minutes or until golden brown and cooked through, turning halfway through. Check the meat is cooked by piercing a thick piece—it should be cooked through with no pink remaining and the juices should run clear.

Eat immediately.

GFC NUGGETS

SERVES 4

PREP TIME: 15 MIN ★ COOK TIME: 14 MIN

WF | GF | DF | NF | SoF

neutral cooking oil

about 2 cups **gluten-free dried bread crumbs**, from a package (NF, SoF if needed)

1 **egg**, beaten, or ⅓ cup **aquafaba** (the water from a can of chickpeas/garbanzo beans, thickened if thin by reducing on the stove—see intro on page 181)

gluten-free all-purpose flour, for dredging

6–8 skinless, boneless **chicken thighs**, cut into nugget-size pieces of about 1½ × ¾ inches (or use **chicken breast**, if you prefer)

salt and **freshly ground black pepper**

Thom's BBQ sauce (see page 191) or Aioli Mayo (see page 188), for dipping

your **favorite sides**, to serve

The gluten-free chicken nuggets in our restaurants are made following a secret recipe. But these are fantastic, too.

Heat the oven to 400°F. Brush a baking pan generously with oil.

Pour about half the bread crumbs into one bowl, the beaten egg or aquafaba into another, and the flour into a third bowl, along with some salt and pepper.

Dip each chicken nugget into the flour, then the egg/aquafaba, and finally the bread crumbs, being sure to cover thoroughly in each coating (and refill the bread crumb bowl as needed). Put the nuggets onto the oiled pan in a single layer.

Bake the nuggets for 14 minutes, turning twice during cooking. When ready, they should be golden brown and crispy, and the meat should be cooked through with no pink, and any juices should run clear.

Serve hot, with sauces for dipping and your favorite sides.

=TIP=

If you only have regular bread crumbs, they will work here, too.

BAKED CHICKEN NUGGETS
WITH AN ALMOND, LEMON & PARSLEY CRUMB

SERVES 4

PREP TIME: 20 MIN　*　COOK TIME: 10–15 MIN

WF | GF | DF | SoF

1 cup **whole, blanched almonds**

2 teaspoons **salt**, or more to taste

1 teaspoon **unwaxed lemon zest**

1 tablespoon minced **fresh flat-leaf parsley**

1 teaspoon **sweet smoked paprika**

½ teaspoon **freshly ground black pepper**

½ teaspoon **cayenne pepper**

½ teaspoon **garlic powder**

2 **eggs**

¾ cup **gluten-free all-purpose flour**

8 large skinless, boneless **chicken thighs**, cut into nugget-size pieces

dipping sauces, to serve (see pages 188–95)

These are another great, healthy, gluten-free alternative to chicken nuggets. Baked not fried, and with an almond crumb instead of the usual breading, they are almost too addictive.

Heat the oven to 400°F. Line a large baking pan with parchment paper.

Put the almonds into a food processor and process until finely ground. Add the salt, lemon zest, parsley, spices, and garlic powder and pulse to combine. Pour into a bowl. Taste and adjust for seasoning. It should be salty—because it's the only seasoning the meat will get—but not overwhelmingly so.

In a second bowl, whisk the eggs until fluffy. Put the flour into a third bowl.

Now set up a nugget assembly line. Dip a chicken piece thoroughly in the flour, shaking off any excess, then dip in the egg, making sure it is completely coated. Finally, dip in the almond mixture, tossing it gently until it is completely covered. Put onto the lined baking pan. Repeat with all the remaining chicken pieces.

Bake for 10–12 minutes or until golden brown and completely cooked, turning halfway through (break open a piece to check that no pink remains). Remove from the oven and serve hot with your choice of sauces.

SPICED-YOGURT CHICKEN WINGS

SERVES 4, WITH SIDE DISHES

PREP TIME: 10 MIN, PLUS MARINATING, IF YOU HAVE TIME * COOK TIME: 30 MIN

WF | GF | NF | SoF

vegetable oil, for greasing

3 heaping tablespoons **Greek yogurt**

1 teaspoon **olive oil**

3 cloves of **garlic**, crushed

1½ teaspoons **sumac** (or zest of
¼ **unwaxed lemon**)

½–1 teaspoon **dried red pepper flakes**,
to taste

1½ teaspoons **ground cumin**

1 tablespoon **paprika**

a pinch of **fennel seeds**, coarsely
pummeled in a pestle and mortar
(optional)

1½ teaspoons **salt**

plenty of **freshly ground black pepper**

12 **free-range chicken wings**

TO SERVE:

Hummus (see pages 186–87)

flatbreads (WF, GF if needed)

your choice of **salad**—try **Baked Paneer
& Warm Chickpeas** (see page 85),
Koshari (see page 89), **Tomato
Kachumber** (see page 103), or **Avocado
& Butter Lettuce** (see page 87)

Deliciously sticky, spiced chicken wings. For a dairy-free version of this recipe, cook the chicken without the marinade. Omit the yogurt and mix the other ingredients to form a dressing, then pour over the hot, cooked wings and toss to serve.

Grease a large metal baking pan with vegetable oil, one big enough to take the wings in a single layer (or use two pans).

In a large bowl, mix together the yogurt, olive oil, garlic, spices, and the generous doses of salt and pepper. Add the chicken wings to the bowl and use your hands to work the thick, spiced marinade into each one. The aim is to coat each one lightly but thoroughly.

If you have time, cover the dish and refrigerate to marinate for an hour or two. If not, you can cook it immediately, in which case heat the oven to 400°F.

Spread out the wings in the prepared pan(s) and cook in the oven for 30 minutes, basting once or twice with the pan juices (add a little more oil to the pan, if there aren't enough juices). The wings are ready when they are golden brown on the outside and, if you pierce one to the bone, the juices run clear.

Serve hot with a big, hearty salad, some hummus, and flatbreads.

EASY JERK CHICKEN

SERVES 4–6

PREP TIME: 10 MIN, PLUS MARINATING * COOK TIME: 15–45 MIN

GF | WF | DF | NF

12 skin-on, bone-in **chicken thighs**
  (or **chicken legs**)

lime wedges, for squeezing

Coconut Rice & Peas (see page 178),
  to serve

FOR THE JERK MARINADE:

a bunch of **scallions**, coarsely chopped

1 small **onion**, coarsely chopped

1¼-inch piece of **fresh ginger**, peeled and
  coarsely chopped

4 cloves of **garlic**, peeled

2 **Scotch bonnet chilies**

3 tablespoons packed **light brown sugar**

1 tablespoon **ground allspice**

1 tablespoon **freshly ground black pepper**

1 teaspoon **freshly grated nutmeg**

1 teaspoon **ground cinnamon**

1 teaspoon **dried thyme**

1 teaspoon **salt**

zest and juice of 1 **unwaxed lime**

2 tablespoons **vegetable oil**

2 tablespoons **soy sauce** (WF, GF if needed)

This is our take on the classic Jamaican dish. A quick-and-easy marinade that can be rubbed over almost anything, including fish or roastable vegetables.

To make the marinade, put all the ingredients into a food processor and blend to make a paste. If it is struggling to blend, turn it off, scrape down the sides, and blend again. Keep doing this until you have a thick, fragrant paste. Taste it for seasoning and adjust accordingly.

Lightly score the skin on the chicken and rub the marinade all over. Put into a bowl, cover, and refrigerate overnight.

The next day, either bake the chicken in a baking pan in a heated oven at 350°F for 40–45 minutes, until the skin is crispy and the meat is cooked through, or cook on a heated hot barbecue grill or broiler pan in a heated broiler for 15–20 minutes, turning once. Check a thick piece to see if the meat is done and the juices run clear. Serve with the coconut rice and peas, with lime wedges for squeezing over the top.

=TIP=

The (unused) marinade will keep in an airtight container in the refrigerator for up to a week.

SIDES, SAUCES & RUBS

═TIP═

You can use this
method and spice
coating on all kinds of
root vegetables, such
as parsnips or carrots.

CRISPY BAKED FRIES

SERVES 4

PREP TIME: 10 MIN * COOK TIME: 40 MIN

WF | GF | DF | V | Ve | NF | SoF

3 large **potatoes** (about 1½ lb), peeled and cut into ¼-inch-thick fries

3 tablespoons **neutral cooking oil**, plus extra for greasing

1 heaping tablespoon **rice flour**

1 tablespoon **semolina**

½ teaspoon **garlic powder**

a pinch of **cayenne pepper** (optional, omit if cooking for small kids)

salt and **freshly ground black pepper**

Crispy fries, but with only a dash of oil. (We've found the holy grail.)

Bring a large saucepan of salted water to a boil, add the potatoes, and parboil for 6 minutes. Drain, spread out in a single layer on a tray, and let dry as much as possible.

Heat the oven to 400°F. Grease two large baking pans. In a large bowl, mix together the remaining ingredients. Gently add the fries and coat. Spread out the fries in the baking pans in a single layer. Bake for 20 minutes, then turn the fries. Return to the oven for another 7–12 minutes or until golden and crisp.

SWEET POTATO WEDGES WITH A CORNMEAL CRUST

SERVES 4–6

PREP TIME: 5 MIN * COOK TIME: 35–45 MIN

WF | GF | DF | V | Ve | NF | SoF

2¼ lb **sweet potatoes**, scrubbed (not peeled) and cut into wedges

¼ cup **olive oil**

1 tablespoon **smoked paprika**

2 teaspoons **garlic powder**

2 tablespoons **cornmeal**

2 teaspoons **salt**

8 twists of **freshly ground black pepper**

Rebecca's friend Grazka put us onto the idea of a cornmeal coating for extra crispiness, and it's a winner.

Heat the oven to 400°F. In a large bowl, mix together the sweet potatoes with half the olive oil and the remaining ingredients. Transfer the coated wedges onto two baking pans and spread out. Drizzle with the remaining oil.

Roast for 35–45 minutes, shaking the pans once or twice, until tender and crisp.

VEGETARIAN NACHOS

SERVES 4–6

PREP TIME: 5 MIN * COOK TIME: 45 MIN

V | NF | SoF

FOR THE REFRIED BEANS:
2 tablespoons **olive oil**

1 **onion**, diced

a small bunch of **fresh cilantro**, stems finely chopped, leaves finely chopped

3 large cloves of **garlic**, minced

½ teaspoon **ground cumin**

1 teaspoon **salt**

10 twists of **freshly ground black pepper**

1 teaspoon **crushed dried ancho chilies**

a pinch of **cayenne pepper**

2 (15-oz) cans **red kidney beans** or **pinto beans**, drained and rinsed

zest and juice of 1 **unwaxed lime**

1 tablespoon **butter**

FOR THE NACHOS:
about 1 (10-oz) package of sturdy **tortilla chips**

1⅓ cups shredded **cheddar cheese**

⅔ cup crumbled **feta cheese**

TO SERVE:
⅔ cup **sour cream** (optional)

Guacamole (see page 195)

4 **scallions**, finely chopped

4 **radishes**, thinly sliced

2 **red chilies**, thinly sliced

fresh cilantro leaves

lime wedges

Pretend it's the Super Bowl every day. This is a hearty, healthy, tasty platter that will satisfy appetites on any occasion. We love bubbly, crispy, oven-melted cheese any time. Pair with Kentucky Fried Cauliflower (see page 132), LEON Jack Wings (page 134), or any of our nuggets or burgers.

For the refried beans, heat the oil in a wide, heavy saucepan over medium heat. Add the onion and cilantro stems and cook for about 8 minutes, until softened. Add the garlic, cumin, salt, black pepper, ancho dried red pepper flakes, and cayenne pepper and cook for another 5 minutes, until fragrant.

Add the beans to the pan along with a small splash of water and cook, covered, for 20 minutes, until well softened.

Remove the lid, reduce the heat, and mash about three-quarters of the beans with a potato masher. Add the lime zest and juice, butter, and chopped cilantro leaves, stir thoroughly, then cook for another minute or so. Taste and adjust for seasoning, then remove from the heat and cover to keep warm.

Heat the oven to 400°F.

For the nachos, in a large baking pan, lay out the tortilla chips. Spread the refried beans over them (you probably won't need all of them, but add as much as you want), cheddar cheese, and feta cheese. Bake for 10–12 minutes or until the cheeses have melted.

Remove from the oven and top with the sour cream, guacamole, scallions, radishes, chilies, and cilantro leaves. Serve with lime wedges on the side.

THAI BBQ CORN ON THE COB

SERVES 6

PREP TIME: 5 MIN ✳ COOK TIME: 20–30 MIN

WF | DF | V | Ve | SoF

1⅔ cups **unsweetened coconut cream** or **coconut milk**

1 teaspoon **white superfine sugar**

½ teaspoon **salt**

zest of ½ **unwaxed lime** (cut the lime into wedges after zesting, for serving)

1 **pandan leaf**, fresh or frozen

½ cup **lightly salted, dry-roasted peanuts**

vegetable oil, for greasing

6 **ears of corn**, leaves tied back and silks removed

a handful of **fresh cilantro leaves**, finely chopped

Inspired by a recipe from legendary Thai-cuisine chef Andy Ricker, the ears of corn can be broiled if you don't want to barbecue. Pandan leaves are available, fresh or frozen, from Chinese grocery stores or online.

Heat the barbecue grill or broiler to high.

Combine the coconut cream or milk, sugar, salt, lime zest, and pandan leaf in a saucepan over high heat. Bring the mixture to a boil, then reduce to a simmer. Cook for 10–15 minutes, until it has thickened slightly. Discard the pandan leaf and set aside the mixture.

In a food processor, pulse the peanuts until they become the texture of coarse bread crumbs. Set aside.

Oil the grate or rack and place the ears of corn in the middle. Close the lid (if your grill has one—if not, you can use aluminum foil to capture some of the heat) and cook or broil for 10–15 minutes, turning regularly and basting the cobs with the coconut cream mixture using a pastry brush, until they are cooked through and slightly charred.

Once the corn is cooked, spread over any remaining coconut cream mixture, then sprinkle with the chopped peanuts and top with the chopped cilantro. Serve with a lime wedge to squeeze over each cob.

MEXICAN BBQ CORN ON THE COB

SERVES 4
PREP TIME: 5 MIN * COOK TIME: 10–15 MIN
WF | GF | V | NF | SoF

vegetable oil, for greasing

4 large **ears of corn**, leaves tied back and silks removed

3 tablespoons **sour cream**

3 tablespoons good-quality **mayonnaise**

2 cloves of **garlic**, grated

1 teaspoon **smoked paprika**

zest of ½ **unwaxed lime**

1 teaspoon **medium chili powder**

1 teaspoon crushed **dried ancho chilies**

1 teaspoon crushed **dried chipotle chilies**

2 oz **Parmesan cheese** or Mexican **cotija cheese** (or use **vegetarian Parmesan-style cheese**; ⅔ cup grated)

a handful of **fresh cilantro leaves**, chopped

salt and **freshly ground black pepper**

lime wedges, to serve

≡ TIP ≡

If you don't have a barbecue grill, parboil the ears of corn for 4 minutes and then char on a smoking hot ridged grill pan for another 5–6 minutes.

If you've only ever had boiled corn on the cob, this might blow your mind (it blew ours). The smokiness from the barbecue and the tanginess of the coating is unbelievable. It's a popular street food in Mexico, where it's called elote.

PS: LEON diehards might remember when we served corn-off-the-cob in our Canary Wharf restaurant instead of our usual fries (we didn't have enough space to cook fries in our tiny kitchen, but warm, spicy corn worked well as a replacement).

Heat the barbecue grill to high.

Oil the grate and place the corn cobs in the middle. Close the lid (if your grill has one—if not, you can use aluminum foil to capture some of the heat) and cook for 10–15 minutes, turning regularly, until they are cooked through and slightly charred.

While the cobs are cooking, prepare the coatings. In a small bowl, whisk together the sour cream, mayonnaise, garlic, smoked paprika, and lime zest. Season to taste with a pinch each of salt and pepper.

In a separate small bowl, mix together the three chili powders.

Finely grate the cheese onto a plate large enough to roll the cooked cobs on later.

When the corn is cooked, use a pastry brush to spread over the mayo-sour cream mix. Then roll all sides through the grated Parmesan. Finally, sprinkle with as much chili powder as you can handle and some chopped cilantro leaves.

Squeeze a lime wedge over each one and eat as soon as you think it's cool enough not to burn your mouth.

COCONUT RICE & PEAS

SERVES 4
PREP TIME: 15 MIN ★ COOK TIME: 12 MIN, PLUS STANDING
WF | GF | DF | V | Ve | NF | SoF

1⅓ cups **basmati rice**

1 cup **coconut milk**

1 (15-oz) can **red kidney beans, black beans**, or **pigeon peas**, or a can containing a mix of all 3 beans, drained (reserving the liquid) and rinsed

1 **scallion**, finely chopped

1 **red chili,** with a slit cut down one side

a sprig of **fresh thyme** or a tiny pinch of **dried thyme**

a pinch of **salt** (optional)

freshly ground black pepper

Serve this dish with the Easy Jerk Chicken on page 168. (We first wrote this to go with curry goat in our "Happy Curries" book, but we think it's essential for jerk dishes, too.)

Wash the rice in cold running water and drain. In a large saucepan with a lid, mix together the coconut milk, the liquid from the can of beans (plus a little water as needed to make up to 1 cup), the beans, scallion, chili, thyme, salt (unless the bean liquid was already salted), and some black pepper. Bring to a simmer, then add the washed rice and cover.

Cook for 12 minutes, stirring once or twice at the end of cooking. Remove from the heat and let stand (covered) for 5–8 minutes. Discard the chili.

Fluff up with a fork before serving.

DIRTY RICE

SERVES 4

PREP TIME: 10 MIN * COOK TIME: 40–45 MIN

DF | NF | SoF

1 tablespoon **vegetable oil**

8 oz lean **ground beef**

8 oz good-quality **sausage meat** (nitrite-free, if possible)

1 **onion**, diced

1 **green bell pepper**, seeded and diced

1 **celery stalk**, diced

1 **green chili,** diced

5 cloves of **garlic**, minced

1 tablespoon **Cajun Rub** (see page 196)

1⅔ cups **long-grain white rice**

4 cups hot **chicken broth**

2 **bay leaves**

salt (optional)

3 **scallions**, thinly sliced, to garnish

This dish goes well with the Spiced-Yogurt Chicken Wings on page 167 or anything grilled or broiled (especially the Skirt Steak with Chimichurri on page 106).

Heat the oil in a heavy casserole dish over medium-high heat. Add the ground beef and sausage meat, using a wooden spoon to crumble and break them up, and cook for 8–10 minutes, until well-browned.

Add the onion, green bell pepper, celery, chili, garlic, and spice mix. Cook, stirring, for 6–8 minutes, until softened.

Add the rice, broth, and bay leaves. Bring to a boil, reduce the heat, and simmer, covered, for 20–25 minutes or until the rice is cooked.

Check for seasoning and add some salt, if needed. Garnish with the scallions and serve.

TIP

If you want to turn this dish into a main meal, serve with a fried egg on top of each portion.

≡ TIP ≡

This technique also works for "fried" avocado wedges for tacos as well as for crunchy "fried" tofu.

BAKED TEMPURA EVERYTHING

SERVES 4 AS A NIBBLE OR APPETIZER
PREP TIME: 15 MIN * COOK TIME: 10–25 MIN
DF | NF | SoF

neutral cooking oil, for brushing

up to 2½ cups **gluten-free dried bread crumbs**, from a package

1 **egg**, beaten, or ⅓ cup **aquafaba**

all-purpose flour, for dredging

your choice of some or all of the following:

 20 large **raw peeled shrimp**

 1 **zucchini**, halved and cut into ½-inch-thick wedges

 1 cup trimmed **green beans**

 1 head of **broccoli**, broken into florets

 ½ **butternut squash**, peeled, seeded, and cut into ½-inch wedges

salt and **freshly ground black pepper**

Roasted garlic Mayo (see page 189), for dipping (Ve if needed)

We were really surprised to discover that store-bought, gluten-free bread crumbs crisp up far better in the oven than wheat-based crumbs. If you don't want to use egg, thick aquafaba works well—aquafaba is the water from a can of chickpeas (garbanzo beans), but you need to make sure it's gloopy; if yours is watery, reduce it slightly in a saucepan on the stove and cool before use.

You can do both shrimp and vegetables, or one or the other. Rebecca worked in Lisbon a few years ago, where tempura green beans are famous—she recommends you try them here, too. Whatever you use, these crispy tempura work really well as an alternative to nuggets, or as a fish replacement for the Asian Fish Stick Wrap on page 45.

Heat the oven to 400°F. Brush one or two baking pans (depending on how much/what you're cooking) generously with oil.

Pour about half the bread crumbs into one bowl, the beaten egg or aquafaba into another, and the flour into a third bowl. Season the flour. Dip each tempura piece into the flour, then the egg/aquafaba, and finally the bread crumbs, being sure to coat thoroughly each time. Put onto the oiled pan(s) in a single layer. Refill the bread crumbs as needed.

When ready to cook, put the pan(s) into the oven. Shrimp will take 10 minutes, and should be turned once. Zucchini, beans, and broccoli will take 14–15 minutes, and butternut squash will take 20–25 minutes, to cook through and crisp up, and all should be turned twice.

Serve the crispy tempura with roasted garlic mayo, for dipping.

CHICKPEA PANISSE

SERVES 4–6 GENEROUSLY
PREP TIME: 10 MIN, PLUS COOLING & CHILLING * COOK TIME: 30 MIN
WF | GF | DF | V | Ve | NF | SoF

1 tablespoon **olive oil**, plus extra for greasing and cooking
3 cups **chickpea (besan) flour**, sifted
vegetable oil, for cooking
salt

Chickpea flour, aka besan flour, contains ten times as much protein as potatoes. These panisse, crunchy little puffs of chickpea dough with crispy outsides and fluffy innards, come from Marseille and are a great alternative to French fries, dusted with a little salt, or finely chopped rosemary, or black pepper and lemon zest, or dried red pepper flakes…

Grease a large baking dish with oil. Bring 4 cups of water to just below a simmer in a large saucepan. Add the tablespoon of oil, a pinch of salt, and the flour. Whisk vigorously to form a smooth batter (or remove any lumps with an immersioon blender).

Cook for 5–7 minutes, stirring continuously—otherwise it will form a skin and give you more lumps to deal with. Then pour the batter into the prepared dish and smooth over the top, working quickly, because it will begin to set immediately. Set aside to cool, then refrigerate for 4–24 hours to set. Turn out the set batter onto a cutting board. Use a sharp knife to slice it into thin, finger-size pieces.

When ready to cook, put a wide, heavy skillet over medium heat and pour in a 50:50 mixture of olive oil and vegetable oil to a depth of just under ½ inch. When the oil is shimmering hot, or about 365°F, use tongs to carefully place some of the panisse in the hot oil. Don't overcrowd the pan, otherwise the oil will cool down.

If the panisse in this batch puff up and split, losing their shape a little, reduce the heat—if they do puff up, however, it doesn't affect how they taste. Cook for about 6 minutes in total, turning regularly, until golden brown and really crisp all over.

Remove from the oil and let drain on a plate lined with paper towels. Keep warm in a low oven while you cook the rest.

Serve hot, sprinkled with salt.

=TIP=

You can make these in batches, or cook in advance, and then reheat them for about 5 minutes in the oven. They're great dunked into Aioli Mayo (see page 188).

SIDES, SAUCES & RUBS

QUICK PICKLES

MAKES 3 JARS
PREP TIME: 15 MIN, PLUS COOLING & STORING ★ COOK TIME: 5 MIN
WF | GF | DF | V | Ve | NF | SoF

FOR THE PICKLING SOLUTION (MAKES ENOUGH FOR THREE 12-OZ JARS):

1 cup **white wine vinegar**

½ cup **apple cider vinegar** (Ve if needed)

2 teaspoons **superfine sugar**

3 teaspoons **salt**

FOR PINK PICKLED ONIONS:

1 **red onion**, very finely sliced

FOR PICKLED RADISHES:

5 oz **radishes**, thoroughly washed, each quartered or cut into six

2 cloves of **garlic**, peeled and left whole

FOR DILL PICKLES:

½ **cucumber**, thinly sliced

2 cloves of **garlic**, peeled and left whole

2 tablespoons coarsely chopped **fresh dill leaves**

This recipe makes enough pickling solution for three 12-ounce jars of pickles, so either make one of each kind here, or triple the quantity of whichever is your favorite vegetable. The pickled onions and radishes are perfect for adding tart crunchiness to Mediterranean wraps, salads (see pages 82–103,) and meze dishes, and the pickled dill cucumbers are the best in hamburgers or cheeseburgers as well as fish sandwiches (see pages 46, 49, and 58). Our restaurant pickles are carefully chosen to be sugar free, because we want to minimize hidden sugars—so you can, of course, omit it here, if you want.

PS: These pickles are not probiotic, because they're not fermented from scratch, but onions, garlic, and radishes are all considered prebiotics, which help create a good environment for digestive tract bacteria to thrive, thereby supporting digestive health.

Wash three 12-oz tempered (heatproof) glass screw-top jars with lids, then sterilize by putting them into a dishwasher or simmering water at 180°F until ready to use.

Prepare the vegetables and pack them tightly into their jars, along with the garlic and herbs. Bring all the pickling solution ingredients and 1 cup of water to a boil in a nonreactive saucepan. Remove from the heat.

Divide the hot liquid among the jars and seal immediately with their lids. Let the jars cool, then store somewhere dark. The onions can be used as soon as they're cool, but all the pickles will be best after they've had at least a few days to develop and ideally a week.

Once opened, keep in the refrigerator. Use a clean spoon when taking them from the jar (this will help them to keep longer), leaving the liquid behind.

ROASTED GARLIC HUMMUS

SERVES 4
PREP TIME: 10 MIN * COOK TIME: 1 HOUR
WF | GF | DF | V | Ve | NF | SoF

At LEON, we don't use potassium sorbate in our hummus, which is a preservative often found in store-bought hummus. We just make sure ours is always superfresh.

2 heads of **garlic**
¼ cup **extra virgin olive oil**, plus extra to garnish
1 (15-oz) can of **chickpeas (garbanzo beans)**, drained and rinsed
juice of 1 large **lemon**
3 tablespoons **tahini**
1 teaspoon **ground cumin**

salt and **freshly ground black pepper**

TO GARNISH:
a large handful of **fresh parsley**, chopped
a pinch of **smoked paprika**
a few twists of **freshly ground black pepper**

Heat the oven to 350°F.

Slice the top off each garlic head, exposing the cloves. Drizzle each with a tablespoon of olive oil, season, and wrap in aluminum foil, scrunching the top into the shape of a teardrop. Roast in a baking pan for about 1 hour, until soft and fragrant. Remove from the oven, open the foil, and let cool.

Squeeze the garlic flesh into a food processor. Add the remaining oil, chickpeas, lemon juice, tahini, and cumin and blend until completely smooth. Add more tahini if too thin, a splash of cold water if too thick. Taste for seasoning, adjust, and blend again. Serve garnished with a drizzle of oil, the chopped parsley, smoked paprika, and black pepper.

BEET HUMMUS

SERVES 4
PREP TIME: 10 MIN
WF | GF | DF | V | Ve | NF | SoF

A wonderful, tangy hummus that turns a gorgeous pink thanks to the beets. Don't omit the mint—it makes the dish.

5 **cooked beets** (about 9 oz; if buying store-bought beets, choose ones not in vinegar)
1 clove of **garlic**, minced or grated
1 (15-oz) can of **chickpeas (garbanzo beans)**, drained and rinsed
juice of 1 **lemon**
3 tablespoons **tahini**
1 teaspoon **ground cumin**
¾ teaspoon **ground coriander**

¼ cup **extra virgin olive oil**, plus extra to garnish
salt and **freshly ground black pepper**

TO GARNISH:
a handful of **fresh mint leaves**, chopped
a few twists of **freshly ground black pepper**
a pinch of **cayenne pepper**
a pinch of **poppy seeds**

Process all the ingredients, except the oil (but including salt and pepper to taste), in a food processor until completely smooth (at least 2 full minutes). Then pour in the olive oil in a stream with the blades running for about another minute, until the hummus is light and creamy. Add more tahini if it is too thin. Add a splash of cold water If it is too thick. Taste for seasoning and acidity, adjust, and process again to combine.

Transfer the hummus to a bowl and serve garnished with a drizzle of extra virgin olive oil, the chopped mint, black pepper, cayenne pepper, and poppy seeds.

ROASTED RED PEPPER HUMMUS

SERVES 4
PREP TIME: 10 MIN
WF | GF | DF | V | Ve | SoF

This hummus is deliciously creamy, smoky, and sweet.

2 **roasted red bell peppers from a jar,** drained and rinsed if in a preserving liquid
1 clove of **garlic,** minced or grated
1 (15-oz) can of **chickpeas (garbanzo beans),** drained and rinsed
juice of 1 large **lemon**
3 tablespoons **tahini**
1 teaspoon **sumac**
1 teaspoon **smoked paprika**
¼ teaspoon **cayenne pepper**
¼ cup **extra virgin olive oil,** plus extra to garnish
salt and **freshly ground black pepper**

TO GARNISH:
a pinch of **smoked paprika**
a few twists of **freshly ground black pepper**
a handful of toasted **pine nuts**

Process all the ingredients, except the oil (but including salt and pepper to taste), in a food processor until completely smooth (at least 2 full minutes). Then pour in the olive oil in a stream with the blades running for about another minute, until the hummus is light and creamy. Add more tahini if it is too thin. Add a splash of cold water if it is too thick. Taste for seasoning, adjust, and process briefly again to combine.

Transfer the hummus to a bowl and serve garnished with a drizzle of extra virgin olive oil, the smoked paprika, black pepper, and toasted pine nuts.

AVOCADO & BASIL HUMMUS

SERVES 4
PREP TIME: 10 MIN
WF | GF | DF | V | Ve | NF | SoF

This is earthy, fresh, and a beautiful green color.

2 medium-size ripe **avocados,** peeled and pitted
1 (15-oz) can of **chickpeas (garbanzo beans),** drained and rinsed
a small bunch of **fresh basil leaves**
1 clove of **garlic,** minced
3 tablespoons **freshly squeezed lime juice**
3 tablespoons **tahini**
1 teaspoon **ground cumin**
1 teaspoon **sumac**
¼ cup **extra virgin olive oil,** plus extra to garnish
salt and **freshly ground black pepper**

TO GARNISH:
a large handful of **fresh parsley leaves,** chopped
a pinch of **dried red pepper flakes**
a few twists of **freshly ground black pepper**
a handful of **pumpkin seeds**

Process all the ingredients, except the oil (but including salt and pepper to taste), in a food processor until completely smooth. Then pour in the olive oil in a stream with the blades running until the hummus is light and creamy. Add more tahini if it is too thin, a splash of cold water if too thick. Taste for seasoning, adjust, and process briefly again to combine.

Transfer the hummus to a bowl and serve garnished with a drizzle of extra virgin olive oil, the parsley, red pepper flakes, black pepper, and pumpkin seeds.

AIOLI MAYO

SERVES 4

PREP TIME: 5 MIN

WF | GF | DF | V | NF | SoF

generous ¼ cup good-quality **mayonnaise** (Ve if needed)
1 small clove of **garlic**, crushed

½ teaspoon **Dijon mustard**
1 teaspoon **extra virgin olive oil**

Mix everything together in a bowl, then taste and add more garlic, mustard, or oil if you want a stronger flavor.

LEON TARRAGON MAYO

SERVES 4

PREP TIME: 5 MIN

WF | GF | DF | V | NF | SoF

⅓ cup good-quality **mayonnaise** (Ve if needed)
1½ tablespoons finely chopped **fresh tarragon**

1½–2½ teaspoons **Dijon mustard**
2 teaspoons **freshly squeezed lemon juice**, or more to taste
2 teaspoons **extra virgin olive oil**, or more to taste

Whisk all the ingredients together in a small bowl. Taste and add more mustard, lemon juice, or oil, if needed.

SRIRACHA MAYO

SERVES 6

PREP TIME: 5 MIN

DF | V | NF | SoF

This is an addictively tasty condiment that can be served with Thai-Spiced Corn Burgers (see page 15), LEON Jack Wings (see page 134), Baked Tempura (see page 181), or any of the nuggets on pages 163–64.

generous ¾ cup good-quality **mayonnaise** (Ve if needed)
3 tablespoons **Sriracha sauce**

2 tablespoons **freshly squeezed lemon juice**
1 clove of **garlic**, grated
salt

Mix all the ingredients together in a bowl until pink and creamy, adding salt to taste. Check the seasoning, adjust if necessary, and mix again, then serve.

ROASTED GARLIC MAYO

SERVES 6

PREP TIME: 5 MIN, PLUS COOLING & CHILLING

COOK TIME: 1 HOUR

WF | GF | DF | V | NF | SoF

Jack's roommate Gordon introduced him to the joys of roasted garlic (he enjoys it squeezed onto hot buttered toast). This is a rich, punchier version of aioli.

1 large head of **garlic**

1 tablespoon **olive oil**

⅔ cup good-quality **mayonnaise** (Ve if needed)

1 teaspoon **freshly squeezed lemon juice**

½ teaspoon **cayenne pepper**

salt and **freshly ground black pepper**

Heat the oven to 350°F.

Slice the top off the head of garlic, exposing the cloves. Drizzle with the oil, season, and wrap in aluminum foil, scrunching the top into the shape of a teardrop.

Put into a baking pan and roast for about an hour, or until the garlic feels soft when pressed.

Remove from the oven, open the foil, and let cool before squeezing the roasted cloves of garlic out of their papery skins into a bowl. Mash with a fork. Add the mayonnaise, lemon juice, cayenne pepper, and salt and pepper to taste and mix until combined.

Cover and refrigerate for about 30 minutes to let the flavors get to know each other before serving.

CAROLINA MUSTARD MAYO

SERVES 4

PREP TIME: 5 MIN

WF | GF | DF | V | NF | SoF

We use this in our LOVe At-Home Vegan Burger (see page 12).

⅓ cup good-quality **mayonnaise** (Ve if needed)

1 teaspoon **yellow mustard**

1 teaspoon **dry English mustard**, or 1½–2 teaspoons **wet English mustard**

a pinch of **salt**

a generous pinch of **cayenne pepper**

½ teaspoon **Worcestershire sauce** (V, Ve if needed)

scant ¼ teaspoon **light corn syrup** or **agave nectar**

½ teaspoon **apple cider vinegar** (Ve if needed)

Mix all the ingredients together in a bowl, then serve.

TIP

All these mayos will keep in the refrigerator in an airtight container for 3 days.

CHIPOTLE MAYO

SERVES 4
PREP TIME: 5 MIN
WF | GF | DF | V | Ve | NF | SoF

This works great with nuggets (see pages 163–64), wings (see page 167), or Jack Wings (see page 134), in LEON's Chicken Burger (see page 19), or even in the LOVe At-Home Vegan Burger (see page 12), if you use vegan mayo. Try using Korean gochujang or American Buffalo-wing-style hot sauce, depending on what you are serving it with.

generous ¼ cup good-quality **mayonnaise** (Ve if needed)

1 teaspoon **chipotle paste** (or more, to taste)

Stir together the mayo and chipotle paste in a small bowl until smooth. If using vegan mayo, it may thin slightly, in which case return to the refrigerator to thicken before serving.

VEGAN MAYO

SERVES 4
PREP TIME: 5 MIN
WF | GF | DF | V | Ve | NF | SoF

This works in place of nonvegan mayo anywhere that it is mentioned in this book. A pinch of Indian black salt, which tastes eggy, makes it even more like traditional mayo.

3 tablespoons **thick aquafaba**

2 teaspoons **vegan apple cider vinegar**

1 teaspoon **freshly squeezed lemon juice**

a generous pinch of **salt**

¾ teaspoon **dry English mustard**

5 **canned chickpeas**

⅔ cup **neutral cooking oil**

Aquafaba is the liquid from a can of chickpeas (garbanzo beans). If yours is thin and watery, reduce it on the stove until it thickens, then cool.

Put all the ingredients, except the oil, into the immersion blender's jar or a bowl. Blend until smooth and pale.

Next, slowly drizzle the oil into the container, blending all the time. It may take a few minutes, but the mixture should eventually start to thicken and turn creamy. (If it doesn't, try a different brand of chickpeas. Use what you have to make a creamy salad dressing, instead.)

You can store in a clean airtight container in the refrigerator for up to 5 days.

SIDES, SAUCES & RUBS

THOM'S BBQ SAUCE

MAKES 1 CUP
PREP TIME: 5 MIN * COOK TIME: 12 MIN

WF | GF | DF | V | Ve | NF | SoF

We crowd-sauced the choosing of this, polling our followers about what our next restaurant sauce should be. We got tens of thousands of submissions, and BBQ sauce was the clear winner. The final recipe was created by Thom Malley, from LEON's food team.

1 cup **ketchup**
¼ cup firmly packed **light brown sugar**
2 tablespoons **apple cider vinegar** (Ve if needed)

1 teaspoon **sweet smoked paprika**
2 cloves of **garlic**, crushed to a paste with the flat of a knife blade
2 teaspoons **liquid smoke salt**

Put the ketchup and sugar into a small saucepan set over medium heat. Stir to dissolve the sugar, then add all the other ingredients, adding salt to taste. Simmer gently for 10 minutes or until thick and dark.

Let cool before serving.

CHIMICHURRI

SERVES 6
PREP TIME: 10–15 MIN, PLUS CHILLING

WF | GF | DF | V | Ve | NF | SoF

Here is our take on a traditional Argentinian sauce. It's usually served with steak but is equally delicious spooned over cooked chicken, fish (we love it with sea bass), and vegetables. Avoid the temptation to chop the herbs in a food processor or they will become soggy. It is best made a few hours in advance and chilled in the refrigerator. But remember to remove 20 minutes before serving to let the sauce come up to room temperature.

1 **shallot**, peeled
3 cloves of **garlic**, peeled
1 **red chili**
a small bunch each of **fresh mint, parsley, cilantro, and dill**, finely chopped

3 tablespoons **red wine vinegar**
scant ½ cup **extra virgin olive oil**, plus extra if necessary
zest of ½ **unwaxed lemon**
salt and **freshly ground black pepper**

Finely mince the shallot, garlic, and chili and put into a mixing bowl with the herbs. Add the vinegar, oil, and lemon zest and mix thoroughly. The oil should just cover the herb mixture, so add a little more if necessary. Add salt and pepper to taste.

Cover and refrigerate for at least a few hours before serving. You can store the chimichurri in an airtight container in the refrigerator for up to 5 days.

LEON TAMARIND KETCHUP

MAKES 1 (8-OZ) JAR OR BOTTLE
PREP TIME: 5 MIN, PLUS COOLING * COOK TIME: 20 MIN
WF | GF | DF | V | Ve | NF | SoF

¼ cup **superfine sugar**
1 tablespoon **tamarind concentrate**
½ teaspoon **ginger puree**
1 tablespoon **pomegranate molasses**
2 teaspoons **white wine vinegar**
¼ teaspoon **ground cumin**
½ teaspoon **garlic powder**
a generous pinch of **cayenne pepper**
a pinch of **ground fennel** or **fennel seeds**
1 tablespoon **molasses**
½ teaspoon **fine salt**
1 tablespoon **cornstarch**

We serve this sauce alongside our GFC nuggets (see page 163) in our restaurants, but you can have it anywhere you like—it's good as an addition to the Beet, Carrot & Onion Bhaji Burgers (see page 20), or when you want a darker, richer, stickier alternative to good old ketchup.

Put all the ingredients, except the cornstarch, with scant 1 cup of water into a small saucepan set over medium heat and bring to a boil, stirring to dissolve and mix everything together.

Reduce the heat and simmer for a couple of minutes. (If your tamarind concentrate, ginger puree, or fennel seeds have left sediment in the ketchup, strain it through a strainer into a pitcher, then return it to the pan.)

In a separate bowl, mix together 1 tablespoon of water and the cornstarch until smooth. Start whisking the ketchup mixture, using a heatproof/pan-safe whisk, and slowly add the cornstarch mix. Keep whisking and turn the heat up to bring the ketchup back to a bubbling boil. When thickened, remove and set aside to cool—it will thicken up some more, so don't worry if it's a little loose. When cool, serve/use as required.

Alternatively, if you plan to keep it for a while, while still hot, pour the ketchup into a clean, sterilized tempered/heatproof glass jar or bottle, with a lid, and seal, then let cool. When opened, store in the refrigerator and use within 2 months.

TARTAR SAUCE

MAKES SCANT ½ CUP

PREP TIME: 5 MIN

WF | GF | DF | V | Ve | NF | SoF

If you love our restaurant fish stick wraps, you can make your own with this sauce, good-quality fish sticks (or veggie alternatives), Gem lettuce, and cucumber.

generous ¼ cup good-quality **mayonnaise** (Ve if needed)

1 tablespoon **capers** in vinegar or brine, rinsed, drained, and coarsely chopped

1 tablespoon finely chopped **shallot**

1 tablespoon finely chopped **Dill Pickles** (see page 185) or store-bought **pickles**

1 tablespoon finely chopped **fresh parsley**

salt and **freshly ground black pepper**

Stir all the ingredients, except the seasoning, together in a bowl, then taste and add salt and pepper—if the pickles are salty, you may not need to add salt. For a sharper sauce, add a squeeze of fresh lemon juice; for a fresher, greener flavor, add 1 tablespoon finely chopped fresh dill and/or tarragon.

Serve immediately or store in the refrigerator in an airtight container for up to 3 days.

LEON BURGER SAUCE

MAKES ENOUGH FOR 4 BURGERS

PREP TIME: 5 MIN

WF | GF | DF | V | Ve | NF | SoF

We originally created this burger sauce for our LOVe Vegan Burger (see page 12) and have been using it on everything ever since. The dill makes it a great accompaniment for salmon, and it's a good dip for potato chips or veggies.

⅓ cup good-quality **mayonnaise** (Ve if needed)

½ teaspoon **garlic powder** (or use 1 small clove of **garlic**, crushed to a paste)

1 teaspoon **yellow mustard**

½ teaspoon **freshly squeezed lemon juice**

½ teaspoon **tomato paste**

2 teaspoons finely chopped **fresh dill**

scant ¼ teaspoon **light corn syrup** or **agave nectar**

a generous pinch of **cayenne pepper**

a pinch of **salt**

Mix all the ingredients together in a bowl.

Serve immediately or store in the refrigerator in an airtight container for up to 3 days.

TZATZIKI

MAKES 1 CUP
PREP TIME: 10 MIN, PLUS DRAINING
& CHILLING
WF | GF | V | NF | SoF

Use in the Spiced Lamb Burger (see page 16), Falafel & Harissa Wraps (see page 26), or serve alongside Spiced-Yogurt Chicken Wings (see page 167), or as a sauce for nuggets.

1 cup **plain yogurt**, Greek if possible

8-inch chunk of **cucumber**

2 cloves of **garlic**, crushed to a paste

1 tablespoon finely chopped **fresh dill** (and/or

1 tablespoon **fresh mint**, if you prefer)

½ teaspoon **freshly squeezed lemon juice**, or to taste

2 tablespoons **extra virgin olive oil**

salt

Line a colander with paper towels or cheesecloth, set it over a bowl, and pour in the yogurt. Let drain for up to 2 hours to thicken the yogurt (in the refrigerator if possible).

Grate the cucumber and squeeze out as much of the liquid as you can, then put it and the drained yogurt into a bowl. Mix in the rest of the ingredients, including a generous pinch of salt. If you can, cover and let the flavors develop for an hour or two in the refrigerator, or even until the next day, because the garlic will mellow. Add more lemon juice or salt, as needed.

Serve immediately or store in the refrigerator in an airtight container for up to 3 days.

GARLICKY YOGURT

MAKES ½ CUP
PREP TIME: 5 MIN, PLUS CHILLING
WF | GF | V | NF | SoF

This is also great served with a little paprika (smoked or not) sprinkled on top. For a thicker sauce, use 1 cup of yogurt and strain it (see Tzatziki recipe, left) before use.

1 clove of **garlic**, crushed to a paste

½ cup **plain yogurt**

a pinch of **salt**

Stir the garlic into the yogurt in a bowl and add the salt. Cover and refrigerate for an hour or two, if you can, to let the flavors develop, then serve or store in an airtight container in the refrigerator for up to 3 days.

GUACAMOLE

SERVES 4
PREP TIME: 5 MIN
WF | GF | DF | V | Ve | NF | SoF

Guac is the quintessential Mexican accompaniment, but we have a soft spot for smearing into burgers, as well as into our tacos and wraps.

1 clove of **garlic**, crushed

1 hot or medium **red chili**, seeded and finely chopped

2 **scallions** or 1 small **shallot**, minced

2 **avocados**, peeled, pitted, and cut into chunks

2 tablespoons finely chopped **fresh cilantro**

juice of ½ **lime** (unwaxed if using zest), plus a pinch of its zest (optional)

salt and **freshly ground black pepper**

Put all the ingredients into a bowl and coarsely mash together, adding salt and pepper to taste—the best guacamole is textured, not smooth. Taste and add more salt or lime juice, if needed. Serve immediately.

PICO DE GALLO

SERVES 4
PREP TIME: 5 MIN
WF | GF | DF | V | Ve | NF | SoF

Effectively a raw relish, this tart combo of crunch and sour brings little bursts of freshness to whatever you sprinkle it over or into. It's good almost anywhere you would use guacamole or sour cream.

2⅓ cups seeded and finely chopped ripe **tomatoes**

2 **shallots**, finely chopped

juice of ½ **lime**

½ **red chili**, seeded and finely chopped

1 tablespoon finely chopped **fresh cilantro**

a pinch of **salt**

Mix all the ingredients together in a bowl. Taste and add more salt as needed.

Serve immediately or store in the refrigerator in an airtight container for up to 3 days.

CAJUN RUB

SERVES 4

PREP TIME: 5 MIN

WF | GF | DF | V | Ve | NF | SoF

1 teaspoon **garlic powder**

a pinch of **dried thyme**

¼ teaspoon **dried oregano**

½ teaspoon **ground cumin**

½ teaspoon **paprika**

a pinch of **cayenne pepper**, or
   to taste

¼ teaspoon **freshly ground
   black pepper**

½ teaspoon **mild red pepper
   flakes**

¼ teaspoon **fine salt**

neutral cooking oil

Mix all the ingredients, except the cokking oil, together in
a small bowl.

When ready to use, mix with a little cooking oil before coating
and cooking your meat, fish, tofu, or vegetables.

TANDOORI RUB

SERVES 4

PREP TIME: 5 MIN

WF | GF | DF | V | Ve | NF | SoF

a pinch of **saffron threads**

seeds from 6 **green cardamom
   pods**

1 teaspoon **paprika**

½ teaspoon **ground coriander**

¼ teaspoon **ground cumin**

¼ teaspoon **ground cinnamon**

a pinch of **cayenne pepper**

a pinch of **ground cloves**

¼ teaspoon **salt**

neutral cooking oil

Grind the saffron threads and cardamom seeds to a
coarse powder using a mortar and pestle. Add all the other
ingredients, except the oil, and mix well.

When ready to use, mix with a little cooking oil before coating
and cooking your meat, fish, tofu, or vegetables.

=TIP=

Each of these recipes
makes enough to
coat 4 servings of
chicken, fish, tofu, or
vegetables.

LEBANESE 7-SPICE RUB

SERVES 4

PREP TIME: 5 MIN

WF | GF | DF | V | Ve | NF | SoF

¼ teaspoon **freshly ground black pepper**

1 teaspoon **ground allspice**

1 teaspoon **ground cinnamon**

1 teaspoon **ground ginger**

1 teaspoon **ground coriander**

½ teaspoon **ground cloves**

½ teaspoon **freshly grated nutmeg**

¼ teaspoon **salt**

neutral cooking oil

Mix all the ingredients, except the cooking oil, together in a small bowl.

When ready to use, mix with a little cooking oil before coating and cooking your meat, fish, tofu, or vegetables.

RAS EL HANOUT RUB

SERVES 4

PREP TIME: 5 MIN

WF | GF | DF | V | Ve | NF | SoF

¼ teaspoon **ground ginger**

¼ teaspoon **hot chili powder**

¼ teaspoon **ground coriander**

¼ teaspoon **freshly ground black pepper**

¼ teaspoon **paprika**

¼ teaspoon **ground turmeric**

a pinch of **ground fenugreek**

a pinch of **ground cinnamon**

¼ teaspoon **ground mace**

a pinch of **ground allspice**

seeds from 8 **green cardamom pods**, ground to a powder

¼ teaspoon **ground cumin**

neutral cooking oil

Mix all the ingredients, except the cooking oil, together in a small bowl.

When ready to use, mix with a little cooking oil before coating and cooking your meat, fish, tofu, or vegetables.

≡TIP≡

These will all keep, before being mixed with oil, stored in an airtight container and somewhere cool and dark, for several months—but their flavors will gradually fade over time.

SWEETS & SHAKES

SHAKES

Shakes are wonderful, but the enormous portions we are sometimes served are crazy, especially from a sugar and health point of view. Each of these serves one, and we reckon they're a sensible size. We use yogurt with active cultures to max out our chances of introducing vital healthy bacteria to our digestive tract biomes, because they thrive on the plant fiber in the recipes. If you want even more fiber, try adding a spoonful of nut butter, ground oats, oat flour, ground flaxseed, or chia seeds (but do be aware that these will all change the texture of your shake and make it thicker).

STRAWBERRY SHAKE

SERVES 1
PREP TIME: 5 MIN
WF | GF | V |NF | SoF

¾ cup hulled **fresh strawberries** (use frozen if out of season)
½ cup **plain yogurt** (with active cultures)
¼ **banana**, peeled
½–1 teaspoon **agave nectar**, **maple syrup**, or **honey**

Process everything together with a splash of water in a blender, until completely smooth. Add sweetness to taste and a little more water as needed, but be sparing. Pour into a glass and serve.

VEGAN PEACH SHAKE

SERVES 1
PREP TIME: 5 MIN
WF | GF | DF | V | Ve | NF | SoF

Keeping the skin on the peach means you get more fiber and micronutrients, but it will take longer to blend and give it a thicker texture, so it's up to you whether you peel or not.

1 **peach**, pitted and cut into chunks (peeled or not)

juice of ½ **orange**

½ **banana**, peeled

4 **ice cubes**

Process all the ingredients together with a splash of water in a blender until completely smooth. Add a little more water as needed, but be sparing. Pour into a glass and serve.

≡TIP≡

If you want to try adding extra probiotics to your diet, these shakes are a good place to start—Rebecca adds good-quality probiotic powder to these shakes when she makes them for herself and her kids.

SWEETS & SHAKES

VEGAN MANGO COCONUT SHAKE

SERVES 1
PREP TIME: 5 MIN
WF | GF | DF | V | Ve | NF | SoF

Mango and coconut go so well together.
(You can, of course, use dairy yogurt, if you prefer.)

1½ cups coarsely chopped
fresh **mango flesh**

¼ cup **coconut yogurt** (with
active cultures)

4 ice cubes

Process all the ingredients together in a blender until completely smooth. Pour into a glass and serve.

APRICOT & VANILLA SHAKE

SERVES 1
PREP TIME: 5 MIN
WF | GF | V | NF | SoF

3 **fresh apricots**, pitted,
skin on

½ teaspoon **vanilla extract**

1 teaspoon **maple syrup**

3 tablespoons **plain yogurt**
(with active cultures)

Process everything together with a splash of water in a blender until completely smooth. Add a little more water as needed, but be sparing. Pour into a glass and serve.

≡ TIP ≡

In the restaurants, we spike this sundae with inulin, a prebiotic that helps good bacteria thrive in the digestive tract. If you want to add it here, you can buy it online, but remember, no more than about ½ teaspoon (and it's not suitable for pregnant women).

MEGHAN'S YOGURT SUNDAE

SERVES 4

PREP TIME: 15 MIN, PLUS COOLING ★ COOK TIME: 10 MIN

WF | V | SoF

FOR THE GRANOLA:
1 cup **rolled oats**
¼ cup chopped **walnuts** or **hazelnuts**
¼ cup chopped **almonds**
3 tablespoons **sunflower seeds**
a generous pinch of **sesame seeds**
1 tablespoon **neutral cooking oil**
1 tablespoon **light corn syrup, agave nectar**, or **honey**
½ cup **dried fruit (raisins, golden raisins, apricots, dates)**, chopped if large

TO SERVE:
½ cup **fruit compote** (see intro)
1¼ cups **thick and creamy plain yogurt**
¾ cup grated or finely chopped **semisweet chocolate**
4 **fresh strawberries**, if in season (optional)

Meghan Rossi is our digestive health guru, and she designed this for the LEON menu. Using yogurt with active cultures introduces good bacteria to the digestive tract, and plant fiber helps it to thrive. Recent research has shown that having a healthy digestive tract biome is key to both physical and mental health.

To make compote from scratch, put a generous 1 cup fresh or frozen berries (raspberries, strawberries, blackberries, or a mixture), chopped if large, into a small, nonreactive saucepan with a splash of water and cook over low heat until the fruit just begins to lose its shape and release its juice. Add a tablespoon or less of sugar, to taste. Cool, then store, covered or in a jar, in the refrigerator for up to 2–3 days.

To make the granola, mix together the oats, nuts, and seeds, then pour the oil and syrup, nectar, or honey over them. Toss really well until everything is coated. Put a wide skillet over low-medium heat and cook the mixture, stirring constantly, for 8–10 minutes, until it smells nutty and toasty and is light gold throughout. If it starts to catch on the bottom of the pan, reduce the heat.

Remove from the heat and transfer to a plate to cool and crisp up. Add the dried fruit and mix. (Any leftovers will keep in an airtight container for about a week.)

When the granola is cool, make the sundaes in 4 glasses. Place a tablespoon of the compote in the bottom of each glass, then add 3 tablespoons of the yogurt. Follow with another tablespoon of compote and 2 tablespoons of yogurt.

Sprinkle one-quarter of the grated chocolate over the yogurt and then cover the chocolate with 2–3 tablespoons of granola or until it is completely covered. Finish each with a fresh strawberry, if using. Eat immediately.

BLUEBERRY FROZEN YOGURT

1 cup **plain yogurt** (straight from the refrigerator)

3½ cups **frozen blueberries**

¼–½ cup **white superfine sugar**, depending on the sweetness of the berries

This is a quick and tasty way to make frozen yogurt, inspired by a video of Swedish chef Magnus Nilsson making something similar at home. You can use any frozen berries—blackberries and raspberries are both delicious—but remember to adjust the amount of sugar depending on the tartness of the berries used. Always add slightly less, taste, and add more if needed.

Make sure the yogurt is really cold. Put all the ingredients in a food processor and process for 30 seconds. Remove the lid and taste for sweetness. Adjust as necessary. Process for another 30 seconds.

Spoon into bowls and serve. It is best eaten immediately, because it melts quickly. To freeze, store in a shallow plastic container, or loaf pan, covered, for up to a month.Remove from the freezer 15 minutes before eating.

APPLE PIE

SERVES 4

PREP TIME: 20 MIN * COOK TIME: 40 MIN

V | NF | SoF

3 large **apples**

2 tablespoons **superfine sugar**

¼ teaspoon **ground cinnamon**

1 sheet **ready-to-bake puff pastry dough**

1 **egg**, beaten (or for a vegan pastry wash, mix 1 teaspoon **neutral cooking oil** with 1 tablespoon **plant-based milk** and ½ teaspoon **agave nectar** or **maple syrup**—but check the package to make sure the pastry itself is vegan, if necessary, too)

1 tablespoon **demerara sugar**

ice cream or **frozen yogurt**, to serve

With only 3 tablespoons of added sugar, this pie gets most of the sweetness from fruit and cinnamon. (Use our egg wash alternative, see left, and look for vegan puff pastry to make this vegan.)

Heat the oven to 350°F. Check the pastry dough package to see if it needs to be taken out of the refrigerator or thawed before use.

Peel, core, and finely dice one of the apples, then put into a small saucepan with the superfine sugar, cinnamon, and 1 tablespoon of water. Bring to a simmer, then cook for about 8 minutes, until soft. Mash to a smooth puree.

Meanwhile, place a piece of parchment paper in a baking pan and place the sheet of pastry dough on top. Cut about one-third of the dough off and return it to the refrigerator. Roll the edges inward to form a lip, about ½ inch deep, all around the remaining sheet of dough. Prick the dough (but not the rim) all over with a fork. Brush with the beaten egg or vegan wash, then bake for 15 minutes. (Reserve the remaining egg or vegan wash for later.)

Halve the remaining apples and cut away the cores and stems. Finely slice into semicircles about 1/16 inch thick.

When the pastry is ready, remove from the oven and gently press down with a spatula if it has puffed up in the middle. Spread the apple puree over the pastry crust, avoiding the rim. Arrange the apple slices on top so they overlap each other in two neat rows. Don't lay them upright or tightly packed, otherwise they won't cook through.

Remove the leftover dough from the refrigerator and cut it lengthwise into six even strips. Lay the strips across the pie in a lattice shape so that each strip interlaces with the strips going in the other direction.

Brush all the exposed dough with the remaining egg or vegan wash, and dab a little under each strip where it joins the rim to hold them in place while cooking. Sprinkle the demerara sugar over the whole pie, and return to the oven to bake for 20–25 minutes, or until the pastry is deep golden and crisp on top, and the bottom is golden, crisp, and looks flaky.

Remove from the oven and eat warm, with ice cream or frozen yogurt.

BAKED VEGAN CHOCOLATE DOUGHNUTS

MAKES 8, PLUS LEFTOVER HOLES

PREP TIME:20 MIN, PLUS RISING * COOK TIME: 9 MIN

DF | V | Ve | NF | SoF

FOR THE DOUGHNUTS:

2⅓ cups **all-purpose flour**, plus extra
   for dusting

2 teaspoons **active dry yeast**

¼ cup **superfine sugar**

scant ¼ teaspoon **ground cinnamon**

a pinch of **freshly grated nutmeg**

½ teaspoon **vanilla extract**

scant ½ cup **plant-based milk** (NF, SoF if
   needed)

½ cup melted and cooled **vegan butter**
   or **margarine** or **dairy butter** (NF, SoF if
   needed)

¼ teaspoon **fine salt**

1 teaspoon **baking powder**

FOR THE CHOCOLATE GLAZE:

¾ cup **confectioners' sugar**

3 tablespoons **unsweetened cocoa
   powder**

2–3 tablespoons **plant milk** (NF, SoF if
   needed)

½ teaspoon **vanilla extract**

A healthy cross between a doughnut and a sweet roll.

For the doughnuts, mix together the dry ingredients, except for the salt and baking powder, in a bowl, then pour in the wet ingredients with the salt. Mix with a spoon until a shaggy dough forms, then knead by hand for 4–5 minutes. Put back into the bowl, cover with a damp dish towel, and let stand in a warm place for an hour to rise.

When risen, line a large baking pan with parchment paper. Flour a clean work surface and rolling pin. Tip out the dough and squash it down, then sprinkle with the baking powder. Knead it lightly into the dough, then roll to about ¾ inch thick. Cut disks using a 4-inch cookie cutter, and use a 1¼-inch round cutter (or a shot glass) to cut a hole in the center of each disk. Transfer to the lined pan, leaving about an inch between each one. Repeat with the remaining dough (be aware that the doughnuts rolled from scraps may rise unevenly). If you have leftover holes, put them onto the sheet, too. Cover again and set aside in a warm place for another 15 minutes to rise.

Heat the oven to 400°F. Boil some water and place a deep metal baking pan on the bottom shelf of the oven. When ready to cook, first carefully pour enough boiled water into the hot pan to fill it to ¾ inch. Then place the doughnut pan on the shelf above. Bake for 9 minutes. The doughnuts will puff up and turn pale gold. Remove from the oven—they may look underbaked, but if you cook them any longer they will turn into crusty rolls.

While the doughnuts are still warm, make the glaze. Sift the confectioners' sugar and unsweetened cocoa powder into a bowl, then slowly add the milk until you have a thick, glossy glaze. Stir in the vanilla. Put a wire rack over a tray. Use tongs to dip each warm doughnut into the glaze, then place on the wire rack for the glaze to set. Eat as soon as possible, ideally while still warm.

BAKED CHEESECAKE

SERVES 8

PREP TIME: 15 MIN, PLUS COOLING & CHILLING * COOK TIME: 32 MIN

V | NF | SoF

sunflower oil, for greasing

2½ cups crushed **graham crackers** (with a sandlike texture)

1 stick (½ cup) **butter**, melted

a pinch of **salt**

1 **egg white**, lightly beaten

1 cup **fresh seasonal fruit** or chilled **compote** (see intro on page 205), strained for a smooth texture, to serve

FOR THE TOPPING:

2½ cups **cream cheese**, at room temperature

¾ cup **superfine sugar**

zest of ½ **unwaxed lemon**

1 teaspoon **vanilla extract**

1 tablespoon **cornstarch**, sifted

4 **eggs**, at room temperature, lightly beaten

Because this cheesecake cooks relatively quickly, it might crack across the top—but don't worry, just disguise it with plenty of beautiful compote.

Heat the oven to 325°F. Thoroughly grease a deep 18-inchspringform cake pan and line the bottom.

For the crust, mix the cookies, melted butter, and salt, then transfer to the prepared pan. Firmly pat flat and press into the edges of the pan until smooth, firm, and really tightly packed.

Use a pastry brush to thinly spread egg white over the crust. Pour on some or all of the rest of the egg white and brush it out to cover any bare patches.

Cook the crust in the oven for about 10 minutes or until you can no longer see patches of wet egg white.

Meanwhile, thoroughly whisk together all the topping ingredients, except the eggs, scraping down the sides and bottom of the bowl to prevent lumps from forming. Add the eggs and use a wooden spoon to mix them in thoroughly until fully incorporated.

When the crust is ready, remove it from the oven. Put a large metal baking pan on the bottom shelf of the oven and pour in enough boiled water to fill it to about 1¼ inches.

Tap the topping bowl on the counter a few times to knock out any large bubbles. Pour the topping onto the crust and smooth out gently. Place in the now steamy oven and cook for 32 minutes (yes, that precise). The center will still be wobbly and the edges just set and slightly puffed up. Turn off the oven, crack open the oven door slightly, and let cool in the oven for about an hour.

Remove from the oven and cool, in the pan, for about 30 minutes, to room temperature. Run a spatula around the cheesecake before opening the pan, in case it has stuck anywhere. Gently remove the cheesecake from the pan and slide onto a plate, then put it into the refrigerator for an hour or until chilled completely to set firmly.

Top with fresh fruit or chilled compote (or both) and serve in slices. Leftovers will keep in an airtight container in the refrigerator for 2 days.

=TIP=

Don't use low-fat or nondairy cream cheese for this dish, because it won't behave itself when in the oven.

≡ TIP ≡

Make these vegan by using plant-based milk and yogurt, and switch the eggs for 2 flax eggs: soak 2 tablespoons flaxseed in ¼ cup cold water for 5 minutes.

SUPERFRUIT MUFFINS

MAKES 12

PREP TIME: 15 MIN, PLUS COOLING ✳ COOK TIME: 25 MIN

V | SoF

heaping ¾ cup **whole-wheat flour**

1¼ cups **all-purpose white flour**, plus
1 tablespoon for coating the fruit

2 teaspoons **baking powder**

½ teaspoon **baking soda**

a pinch of **fine salt**

⅔–¾ cup **superfine sugar** (depending on
your sweet tooth)

2 tablespoons **rolled oats**

2 tablespoons **sunflower seeds**

2 tablespoons **almond meal** (optional,
omit if NF)

⅓ cup **neutral cooking oil**

⅔ cup **plain yogurt**

scant ½ cup **milk**

2 **eggs**

1 teaspoon **vanilla extract**

1 cup **fresh** or **frozen berries** (blueberries,
blackberries, or raspberries, or
a mixture)

1 tablespoon **granulated sugar**

These whole-wheat muffins are packed with oats, seeds, (optional) almonds,, and fruit. They are perfect for a tasty breakfast, brunch, or healthy snack.

Heat the oven to 400°F. Line a 12-cup muffin pan with muffin liners. Sift the flours, baking powder, baking soda, and salt into a large bowl, add the superfine sugar, oats, seeds, and almond meal, and mix together really well.

Mix all the wet ingredients, except the fruit, together thoroughly in a separate bowl.

Put the fruit into another bowl and add the remaining 1 tablespoon of flour, then toss it gently to coat—this stops the fruit from sinking while the muffins cook.

Mix the dry and wet ingredients together as briskly as you can—but don't overmix, it doesn't need to be smooth. Add the fruit and mix once, gently, so that it doesn't break up or turn the batter purple or pink (unless you want it to).

Divide the batter evenly among the muffin liners, working quickly—the baking soda and yogurt will have started to react and form bubbles in the batter, which you want to take advantage of and cook quickly, for maximum lift. Each muffin liner should be really full.

Sprinkle the granulated sugar over the muffins, then put the pan into the oven and bake for 22–25 minutes. When done, the muffins should be puffed up and golden on top. To check the muffins are cooked, remove one carefully from its liner and check the bottom—it should be just brown. Return to the oven and cook for another couple of minutes if not. When cooked, let cool in the muffin pan for at least 10 minutes before transferring to a wire rack.

Serve at room temperature (they may fall apart if you eat them immediately).

≡ TIP ≡

The cookies will look
squishy when you take
them out, but take them
out anyway—overbaked
cookies will be
too dry.

BETTER COOKIES

MAKES 12–14

PREP TIME: 25 MIN, PLUS COOLING ✻ COOK TIME: 10 MIN

V | SoF

¾ cup **all-purpose flour**

2 tablespoons **almond meal**

2 tablespoons **rolled oats**

⅔ cup **unsweetened cocoa powder**

1 teaspoon **baking powder**

¼ teaspoon **baking soda**

⅓ cup **superfine sugar**

6 tablespoons **butter**, melted and cooled (or for DF, use melted **refined flavorless coconut oil** and a pinch of **fine salt**)

2 **eggs**, beaten

2 teaspoons **vanilla extract**

½ cup chopped **nuts** (we like hazelnuts and almonds—smash them up in a more and pestle if yours are whole)

3½ oz **bittersweet chocolate** (at least 70 percent cocoa solids), chopped into ¼-inch pieces, or ⅔ cup good-quality **bittersweet chocolate chips**

1–2 tablespoons **dairy or plant-based milk** (optional)

flaky sea salt (optional; omit if serving to small children)

These "better cookies" (aka double chocolate chip cookies) can't exactly be described as healthy, but they are healthier than a lot of the cookies out there—with oats and almond meal for fiber (plus a little manganese, vitamin E, and magnesium). And cocoa is rich in antioxidant polyphenols. So they're essentially good for us, right? Right?

Heat the oven to 350°F. Line two baking sheets with parchment paper.

In a large bowl, mix together the flour, almond meal, oats, unsweetened cocoa powder, baking powder, baking soda, and sugar. In another bowl, beat together the cooled melted butter, eggs, and vanilla extract, then pour this mixture into the flour bowl. Add the chopped nuts and chocolate pieces or chocolate chips and stir everything together. If it's stiff and fudgy, add up to 2 tablespoons of milk. The dough should be thick but loose enough to slowly drop off the spoon.

Use a soup spoon to place dollops of the dough onto the prepared baking sheets, spacing them out and leaving about 1½ inches between each, because the cookies will spread out as they cook. Sprinkle with flaky sea salt at this point, if you want.

Bake for 6 minutes, then rotate the baking pans around by 180 degrees so the cookies cook evenly. Bake for another 3 minutes.

The cookies will be soft when they come out of the oven, with a slightly cracked appearance, but they will quickly firm up as they cool.

Leave on the baking sheets to cool a little, then transfer to a wire rack. Eat warm or at room temperature. The cookies will keep in an airtight container for about 3 days.

INDEX

ABOUT THE AUTHORS

JACK BURKE is a London-based writer, actor, and private chef. He spent the summers during his college years cooking and traveling around Italy and France. He first worked with John on the book *Winning Not Fighting*. Jack can often be heard on the radio and is the host of several video series for the LEON website.

REBECCA SEAL has written about food and drink for the *Financial Times*, the *Evening Standard*, the *Observer*, the *Guardian*, *Red*, and *The Sunday Times*. Her cookbooks include *Istanbul: Recipes from the Heart of Turkey* and *Lisbon: Recipes from the Heart of Portugal*, as well as coauthoring *LEON Happy Soups*, *LEON Happy One-pot Cooking*, *LEON Fast Vegan*, and *LEON Happy Curries* with John Vincent. She is one of the food and drink experts on the UK's Channel 4 *Sunday Brunch*. She lives in London with her husband and two small daughters.

JOHN VINCENT is cofounder of LEON, which now has more than 75 restaurants (including in Washington, DC, Amsterdam, Utrecht, and Oslo). He wrote *LEON Naturally Fast Food* with Henry Dimbleby, *LEON Family & Friends* with Kay Plunkett-Hogge, *LEON Happy Salads* and *LEON Fast & Free* with Jane Baxter, and *LEON Happy Soups*, *LEON Happy One-pot Cooking*, *LEON Fast Vegan*, and *LEON Happy Curries* with Rebecca Seal. He thinks that our relationship with food should be positive and joyous and that we need to listen more carefully to our stomach, and eat more good fats and less sugar.

ACKNOWLEDGMENTS

JACK

Thank you John and LEON for your show of faith. Thank you Rebecca for your guidance and expertise. Thank you Auntie Susan for indulging my interest in food at the start. And thank you to my friends, family, and girlfriend for being willing guinea pigs and providing useful feedback: Mom, Dad, Eleanor, Tatiana, Gordon, Henry, Anouk, George, Lizzie, Eli, Grahame, and Alex.

REBECCA

Thanks as ever to John Vincent, LEON, and Octopus for letting me be part of the *Happy* team. Thanks to Jack for his wonderful recipes and writing (and for putting up with me cracking the deadline-whip—and meeting them). Once again, Steve Joyce, photographer extraordinaire (and excellent husband), put together the A team: Sian Henley, Lauren Law, and Tom Groves, assisted by Anna Hiddlepit and Grace Paul. And thanks to all Kemble House Studio's neighbors, who made sure no burger, no fry, no nugget, no cookie went to waste.

JOHN

My thanks go to Rebecca and Jack. At LEON, we ask ourselves two questions before we invite people to work in or with us: are they brilliant and are they people of character? We call it the "brilliant/lovely two by two" (imagine a graph with two axes). Well, Rebecca and Jack are top right on this great graph of life. Creative when they need to be, precise when they need to be. And energizing people to work with when they need to be *and* when they don't need to be.

Rebecca has been my cookbook partner multiple times now (for many good reasons), while Jack is a cookbook virgin. Rebecca has been generous by taking Jack in hand and recognizing him as a wonderful new kid on the culinary block.

As important, thank you so much to all my LEON colleagues. We stand on your shoulders when we write these books, only amplifying the work and genius you apply every day.

PS: Can I recommend a book called *Winning not Fighting* that I have written with my friend and martial arts master Julian? I think you will like it. It is about how we need to redefine success in life and how we achieve it. It is not so much about food, but it might indirectly help you make food faster.

An Hachette UK Company
www.hachette.co.uk

First published in Great Britain in 2020
by Conran Octopus, an imprint of
Octopus Publishing Group Ltd
Carmelite House
50 Victoria Embankment
London EC4Y 0DZ
www.octopusbooks.co.uk

Text copyright © LEON Restaurants 2020
Design and layout copyright © Octopus Publishing Group 2020
Denai's Vegan Patties on page 158 © Denai Moore 2020
Chicken, Chorizo & Shrimp Jambalaya on page 141 © Donald Gunn 2020

Distributed in the US by Hachette Book Group
1290 Avenue of the Americas
4th and 5th Floors, New York, NY 10104

Distributed in Canada by Canadian Manda Group
664 Annette Street, Toronto, Ontario, Canada M6S 2C8

ISBN 978-1-84091-807-6

A CIP catalogue record for this book is available from the
British Library.

Printed and bound in China

10 9 8 7 6 5 4 3 2 1

Photography by Steven Joyce

Publisher: Alison Starling
Creative director: Jonathan Christie
Senior editors: Sophie Elletson and Pauline Bache
Production controller: Emily Noto

Food stylist: Sian Henley
Food stylist assistants: Anna Hiddlepit and Grace Paul
Prop stylist: Lauren Law
Photography assistant: Tom Groves
Designer: Ella Mclean
Copy editor: Anna Sheasby
LEON lead designer: Sean Matthews
LEON head of marketing: Rebecca Di Mambro
Author photo: George Selley
Photography on endpapers courtesy of LEON and Tom Groves

We have endeavored to be as accurate as possible in all the preparation and
cooking times listed in the recipes in this book. However, they are an estimate
based on our own timings during recipe testing and should be taken as only a
guide, not as the literal truth.

Nutrition advice is not absolute. If you feel you require consultation with a
nutritionist, consult your physician for a recommendation.

Standard level spoon measurements are used in all recipes.

Eggs should be large unless otherwise stated and preferably free range or
pasture raised and organic. The U.S. Food and Drug Administrationadvises that
eggs should not be consumed raw. This book contains dishes made with raw or
lightly cooked eggs. It is prudent for more vulnerable people, such as pregnant
and nursing mothers, people with a weakened immune system, the elderly,
babies, and young children to avoid uncooked or lightly cooked dishes made
with eggs. Once prepared, these dishes should be kept refrigerated and used
promptly.

Fresh herbs should be used unless otherwise stated. If unavailable, use dried
herbs as an alternative but halve the quantities stated.

Ovens should be preheated to the specific temperature. All oven temperatures
are for a convection oven. If not using a convection oven, increase the
temperature by 25°F.

This book includes dishes made with nuts and nut derivatives. It is advisable for
customers with known allergic reactions to nuts and nut derivatives and those
who may be potentially vulnerable to these allergies, such as pregnant and
nursing mothers, people with a weakened immune system, the elderly, babies,
and children, to avoid dishes made with nuts and nut oils. It is also prudent to
check the labels of store-bought prepared ingredients for the possible inclusion
of nut derivatives.

Vegetarians should read the ingredients on a cheese label to be sure it is made
with vegetarian rennet.

Not all soy sauce is gluten-free—we use tamari (a gluten-free type of soy sauce),
but check the label if you are unsure.

Remember to check the labels on ingredients to make sure they don't have
hidden refined sugars. Even savory goods can be artificially sweetened, so it's
always best to check the label carefully.